Fabulous Felines

Health and Beauty Secrets
for the Pampered Cat

Sandy Robins

Fabulous Felines
Sandy Robins

Project Team
Editor: Mary E. Grangeia
Copy Editor: Stephanie Fornino
Designer: Stephanie Krautheim
Layout and production: Elizabeth Tunnicliffe
Indexer: Dianne L. Schneider

T.F.H. Publications
President/CEO: Glen S. Axelrod
Executive Vice President: Mark E. Johnson
Publisher: Christopher T. Reggio
Production Manager: Kathy Bontz

T.F.H. Publications, Inc.
One TFH Plaza
Third and Union Avenues
Neptune City, NJ 07753

Printed and bound in China
09 10 11 12 3 5 7 9 8 6 4 2

Library of Congress Cataloging-in-Publication Data
Robins, Sandy.
   Fabulous felines: health and beauty secrets for the pampered cat / Sandy Robins.
      p. cm.
   ISBN 978-0-7938-0665-2 (alk. paper)
   1. Cats--Health. 2. Cats--Grooming. I. Title.
   SF447.R63 2008
   636.8--dc22
                     2008015845

The Leader In Responsible Animal Care For Over 50 Years! ®
www.tfh.com

Table of Contents

Chapter One

Fabulous Fur

There's no such thing as an ugly cat! Whether you have a pedigreed Persian or an adopted stray, whether she is longhaired, shorthaired, black, white, orange, calico, tabby, or a cat words just can't describe, beauty in feline terms is defined as being in tip-top physical condition. And that, as every pet parent knows, starts with fabulous fur.

*I*f we spent as much time meticulously taking care of our own hair and nails as our felines do, we would undoubtedly be labeled vain and narcissistic. After all, the standard feline self-pampering routine is about three hours a day! So why, you're probably asking, do cats need help with their beauty schedule if they are already such wonderfully efficient self-cleaning machines? Well, it takes more than a good licking and a few hairballs deposited on your favorite Oriental rug to keep fur looking fabulous.

First, regular bathing and grooming your cat with specially formulated feline products helps keep shedding under control. Indoor cats, in particular, tend to shed continually because they are exposed to air conditioning and heating. Second, grooming removes dander and external organisms—that's a polite euphemism for fleas and other nasties that may attempt to take up residence in your cat's warm, comfortable fur. Also, keeping your feline free of superfluous fur and dander helps reduce human allergies.

But here's the really big plus: Studies have shown that good grooming, along with a lifestyle that promotes general well-being and alleviates stress and anxiety, helps cats live longer, healthier lives. In the 1970s, the typical feline life span was three to four years. Today, 15 years is considered the average, while many cats may live well into their late teens and even into their twenties if given good care.

One thing is certain: Whatever length of time you are blessed with your cat's wonderful companionship, it's never enough. So if you are one of the millions of pet parents around the world

Studies have shown that good grooming helps cats live longer, healthier lives.

who refers to a feline family member as a fur kid, you naturally have her best interests at heart. Good grooming is simply a launching pad for long-term great health and well-being benefits.

THE DIFFERENCE BETWEEN CATS AND DOGS— AND PEOPLE

These days, many pet parents have a beauty routine for their fur kid that mimics their own regimen. When it comes to hair care, people tend to visit a stylist every four to six weeks for a cut and coloring, and in between appointments, manage their tresses at home using products recommended by the salon. In a similar vein, a growing number of cats have standing appointments with a groomer, with their pet parents taking charge between visits.

Yet despite this growing trend, which is becoming even more popular with the advent of mobile feline groomers, most people still groom their cats themselves. Therefore, the focus of this book is all about giving your feline the star treatment at home, with professional hints and tips to ensure that she's always a glamour puss and camera-ready at a moment's notice.

Also, beyond the physical act of grooming, the time spent together is quality time. And even if your cat isn't one of those chatty felines, she will no doubt voice her appreciation in loud purrs. All this pampering will provide the added benefit of relaxing you, too. It's a win-win situation. So let's get started!

INTRODUCING A BEAUTY ROUTINE

The best advice I can give pet parents is to introduce a beauty routine from the moment that bundle of fur comes into your life so that she learns to tolerate every aspect of pampering and actually enjoys it. However, don't simply grab your favorite bottle of revitalizing shampoo from the bathroom shelf and attempt to work up a lather. Human hair is more acidic than feline fur. Shampoos formulated to balance human pH levels tend to dry out pet hair and skin. And because a cat's skin also has different levels of acidity than that of other household pets, don't use your dog's kiwi-melon shampoo or your rabbit's fragrant strawberry formula on your feline fur kid either.

Regular use of the wrong shampoo can actually cause skin irritations. Even so-called "tearless" and "baby" shampoos can be very irritating to feline skin and eyes.

Apart from having a different hair texture and skin acidity level, there are other biological differences to take into consideration that further endorse why your cat needs her own beauty products.

- ✤ A cat's hair follicles have multiple hair shafts, while human hair follicles have only one shaft. This makes them more prone to blockages and oily buildups.
- ✤ Humans have sweat glands all over the body; cats' sweat glands are limited to the paw

pads and bridge of the nose. This means that they don't build up a sweat after lots of activity the way humans do.

✤ Cats have sebaceous glands all over the body, while these glands are limited to hair and facial areas on humans.

✤ As mentioned earlier, cats shed continually—a side effect of an indoor lifestyle that exposes them to air conditioning and heating. This has a drying effect on skin and fur.

Shedding Facts

Shedding is a normal, natural event in a cat's life. It's how animals remove dead hair from their bodies, replenish their fur, and keep it in top condition. Members of the cat family living in the wild generally shed twice a year: in the spring to lose the heavy winter undercoat and in the fall in preparation for the "grow-in" of the next winters' undercoat. However, your domestic fur kid's indoor lifestyle, especially if there's both air conditioning and heat, will cause her to shed continually. This is because her biological system becomes confused, putting her into a constant state of shedding.

Shedding is largely influenced by daylight, or more specifically the number of hours a cat is exposed to sunlight in a day (called a photoperiod), which is what triggers the shedding process. Also, the amount a cat sheds will vary quite a bit from breed to breed and will also be affected by how often she is groomed, bathed, brushed, etc.

A WORD ABOUT HAIR

To take it a step further, different cats have different hair types. Fortunately, the whole hairy business is not nearly as complicated and varied as it is in dogs. Canines have long silky coats, short wiry coats, curly coats, corded coats, and double coats to complicate their beauty equation.

In beauty terms, fabulous felines are usually classified simply by their obvious visual appearance: longhaired versus shorthaired and hairless. In fact, the only cats who don't fall into these three categories are Rex cats: the Cornish Rex and the Devon Rex. The word "Rex" is shortened from the genetic term asterx, which means the absence of guard hairs—the top hairs that give cats insulation. The Cornish Rex has a short crimped coat with no guard hairs and even has crinkled whiskers, giving him a very stylish impish look. The Devon Rex has guard hairs that vary in length, making the fur look slightly lumpy and giving the effect of a perm that's growing out. And I'm not being catty—these are just visual descriptions for the benefit of readers who are not too familiar with these feline beauties.

Within the categories of longhaired and shorthaired cats, there are minor hair differences that serious cat people will take into consideration when grooming for the show ring, sometimes using different types of shampoos during one bathing session and a variety of products to create a specific look. Generally speaking, grooming for the show ring is a whole different ball of string and not the focus of this health and beauty book.

Now, let's get back on track.

CHOOSING PRODUCTS FOR FABULOUS FUR

While people select hair grooming products according to a particular hair type (such as normal, greasy, or dry), when it comes to choosing everyday products to groom your glamour puss, shampoos are selected by skin type. For example, if you're grooming to maintain already fabulous fur, simply select a shampoo for normal skin. But if your cat shows signs of dry, flaky skin or excessively oily skin, purchase shampoos for these conditions.

Introduce a beauty routine from the moment your cat comes into your life so that she learns to tolerate every aspect of pampering and actually enjoys it.

Despite the fact that cat shampoos are categorized to cater to skin types, it can sometimes be difficult to accurately select the right shampoo and conditioning treatment. It's easy to spot dandruff-like flakes. But does this mean that your pet has dry, flaky skin or dry, flaky, and irritated skin? Cats, like people, are affected by a gamut of things; air pollutants, grass, air conditioning, and heating can all cause your fur kid to develop dry, itchy skin and cause the fur to become matted, static, or oily.

It's also important to mention that feline skin and fur-related problems compose the largest percentage of visits to the veterinarian and are often indicators of internal problems. Basically, this means that even a specially formulated shampoo may be treating the symptoms and not the cause of the problem. So if your feline has signs of a skin condition and you're in doubt, make an appointment with your veterinarian instead of seeking over-the-counter product advice at the pet boutique or supermarket. If there is no underlying medical condition affecting her skin and fur, it's a good idea to consult with a professional cat groomer for advice on general coat and skin care needs, as well as information about specific products in accordance with your fur kid's lifestyle.

WHAT TO LOOK FOR ON THE LABEL

Although all cat products are subject to strict control standards, some contain better-quality ingredients than others. Human cosmetic-grade ingredients are obviously more expensive than those termed "chemical grade." There will be clues on the label because any products formulated by veterinary dermatologists or those that contain human-grade ingredients will tout this information.

Here's a guide to key words to look for on labels for specific skin types when touring the feline products aisle.

Dry/Flaky Skin

Dry, flaky skin requires both moisturizing and conditioning. Look for a shampoo containing protein and moisturizing ingredients that will soften and soothe the skin as well as leave the coat shiny and glossy. At best, consider using a shampoo with moisturizing ingredients and follow up with a leave-on moisturizing and conditioning treatment.

Some key words on the label include:

- **Allantoin.** It stimulates the formation of healthy skin and hair tissue, and it soothes itchy skin.
- **Aloe vera.** It has soothing properties.
- **Borage oil.** It is a source of gamma linolenic acid (GLA) and works to eliminate dry, flaky, itchy skin; it also reduces shedding and promotes glossy hair.
- **Oatmeal.** It is a popular ingredient used to soothe dry, sore, and inflamed skin.

When it comes to choosing everyday products with which to groom your glamour puss, shampoos are selected by skin type.

It exfoliates, getting rid of dead skin cells that cause flaking.

- **Hydrolyzed proteins** (such as silk, soy, wheat, and oat proteins). Proteins help increase the skin's ability to hold moisture.
- **Vitamin E.** It is used as a moisturizer.
- **Panthenol (vitamin B5).** It repairs dry, damaged hair.

Dry/Itchy Skin

Dry, itchy, or sore skin needs to be well moisturized and also treated to heal skin irritations. If you reduce itching, it's possible to avoid secondary infections caused by scratching. Despite the fact that cats meticulously manicure their feet, there's dirt under their nails.

Key ingredients to look for in relevant products include:

- **Allantoin.** It stimulates the growth of skin and hair tissue while soothing and healing skin.
- **Coal tar.** It has medicated antibacterial properties.
- **Sulphur.** This is a mineral that has antiseptic properties and is often found in products along with salicylic acid, which is known to reduce the pH of the skin, allowing it to absorb water.
- **Chamomile and comfrey.** These are plant extracts that have wonderful anti-inflammatory and soothing properties.
- **Glycerin.** It has conditioning properties.
- **Oatmeal.** Once again, a firm favorite to soothe dry, sore, and inflamed skin. It exfoliates, getting rid of dead skin cells that cause flaking.

Greasy/Flaky Skin

Key ingredients that reduce oiliness and rejuvenate by slowing down cell activity and by healing the skin include:

- **Refined tar.** This is an antipyretic that stops itchiness, redness, and swelling.
- **Sulphur.** It is used for its soothing therapeutic properties.
- **Salicylic acid.** It helps strip away dead skin.
- **Aloe vera and chamomile.** These plant extracts have excellent antibacterial properties.
- **Zinc gluconate.** It combats oiliness.
- **Ylang-ylang and lavender.** These ingredients control oiliness and have soothing properties.

Shampoo Tip

When in doubt about what shampoo to use, consider an oatmeal-based formula. Oatmeal offers relief for dry, itchy skin and has wonderful conditioning properties that will make hair soft and easily manageable. It's inexpensive and widely available from pet boutiques, supermarkets, and on-line stores.

Allergic Skin

Skin allergies are best treated with a hypoallergenic shampoo. This means that the product has no colorants or fragrance. Look for products that contain:

- ❖ **Allantoin.** It stimulates healthy skin and hair tissue while soothing and healing skin.
- ❖ **Aloe vera.** Apart from its soothing effect, it also has antibacterial properties.
- ❖ **Vitamin E.** It is used as an antioxidant and helps repair skin damage.
- ❖ **Oatmeal.** Once again, it is known for its antibacterial and soothing effects.
- ❖ **Panthenol (vitamin B5).** It repairs damaged skin and hair.

Often labels refer to "hot spots." By definition, hot spots are a bacterial infection caused by an allergic reaction. Cats don't suffer from hot spots on their bodies the way dogs do, but they do get them on the chin in the form of feline acne. Specific medicated shampoos containing hydrocortisone formulated for soothing and treating inflamed spots are available over the counter.

Also look for ingredients such as:

- ❖ **Aloe vera, peppermint, and geranium.** These plant extracts have soothing properties.
- ❖ **Tea tree oil.** It is often included for its antiseptic properties.
- ❖ **Chamomile.** It is an excellent anti-inflammatory.

However, when it comes to skin allergies and hot spots, don't guess—seek veterinary advice.

BOTANICAL SHAMPOOS AND SPA TREATMENTS

Botanicals are products that contain organic herbs, natural plant extracts, and essential oils obtained from plants, leaves, bark, roots, seeds, resins, and flowers such as those used in aromatherapy. They are called spa treatments because apart from their cleansing, moisturizing, and conditioning properties, these ingredients also induce a sense of calm and improve general well-being. Natural plant extracts and essential oils are considered an antidote to a fast-paced, hectic lifestyle for humans. And because grooming and pampering our fur kids are nothing more than extensions of the way we feel about ourselves, these products aim to mimic the same positive effects on our pets.

Note that while standard shampoo and conditioning products contain some aromatherapy ingredients, a true botanical or aromatherapy spa product will only contain natural ingredients and no chemical simulations. However, always check labels to ensure that the products are created specifically for cats because some essential oils are toxic to felines. Having said this, there is a growing controversy as to how beneficial these products really are because the amounts of the natural ingredients used are not stated on the labels, and often the quantities are minimal. But they do smell good!

In particular, look for shampoos and spa products, such as moisturizing and freshening sprays, that include the following botanical extracts:

- ❖ **Chamomile.** It has astringent and soothing properties.
- ❖ **Cactus.** It is a succulent that has moisturizing and conditioning properties.
- ❖ **Calendula and aloe vera.** These plant extracts are known for their healing effects.
- ❖ **Fir needle oil.** It is known to have a wonderfully freshening effect on fur.
- ❖ **Eucalyptus.** It has cooling, refreshing properties and is also a natural respiratory aid.
- ❖ **Lemongrass.** It is a natural energizer, and it invigorates the skin.
- ❖ **Lavender.** It is known for its calming and relaxing properties.
- ❖ **Ylang-ylang.** It is a natural calmative.
- ❖ **Jasmine.** It is known to create an upbeat mood.
- ❖ **Sandalwood.** It has healing properties.

Aromatherapy sprays can be used to spritz your cat and freshen her fur at any time. They are safe to use on pet beds too.

Never add your own essential oils to your cat's shampoo or apply them directly to her skin. Essential oils are very concentrated, and instead of having a positive effect, you could induce a toxic one.

SHAMPOOS FOR FLEAS AND TICKS

Flea and tick shampoos provide some instant help but have no long-term benefits. Because the public is generally uninformed about the effects of insecticides on pets, use of the wrong products can do more harm than good; some insecticides can be toxic to cats and kittens and may even cause death.

Personally, I believe that dealing with fleas and ticks is

Always ensure that any pet product you use is specifically made for cats.

a science. The current trend focuses on topical products, some of which contain insect growth regulators (IGRs) that break the flea's life cycle. Consequently, flea and tick control is a subject to discuss with your veterinarian because he knows your fur kid on a personal level. However, if you are looking for a flea and tick shampoo as an intermediary measure, make doubly sure that you are selecting one that is specifically for cats, and more importantly, safe for kittens if you have a youngster. Never take advice from an uninformed salesperson at the pet store, or worse, simply guess.

GOT SKUNKED?

If your cat has had a smelly encounter with a skunk, there are specially formulated deodorizing shampoos that will remove the odor with one application. Look for products that contain the following:

- **Baking soda.** It is known for its absorptive properties, which eliminate odors.
- **Smellrite.** This is a resin specially processed to absorb and break down foreign odors.
- **Yucca.** It works well to deodorize urine and fecal odors.
- **Lavender.** It is an effective deodorant.

MOISTURIZERS AND CONDITIONERS

Once you have settled on the right shampoo, you are going to need a moisturizer and conditioner for your fur kid, too. Remember, water from a faucet varies greatly from state to state, and "hard" water will affect the texture of your pet's hair in the same way it does yours, making it dry or unmanageable.

All moisturizers work to add moisture and rehydrate the skin and hair follicles. Key ingredients to look for are:

- **Lactic acid.** It improves the skin's ability to retain moisture and is also a natural exfoliant, promoting the production of new skin cells.
- **Glycerine (glycerol).** It has excellent moisturizing properties to prevent skin dryness and is particularly good for treating sensitive or easily irritated skin.
- **Elastin.** This is a key protein ingredient that helps the skin retain moisture, which helps repair damaged hair.
- **Lanolin.** It softens and protects the skin.
- **Panthenol (vitamin B5).** It has moisturizing and conditioning properties that promote hair growth and make hair tangle-free.
- **Diazolidinyl urea.** It helps control the growth of bacteria and other microorganisms.
- **Vitamin E linoleate.** It has antioxidant and skin repair properties.

*Applying a conditioner to your cat's coat will keep it shiny and fluffy
and help prevent fur from matting.*

Conditioners are a combination of ingredients that coat the hair to make it shiny, glossy, and fluffy. They prevent static and also stop fur from matting and tangling. The labels are pretty specific, so they are much easier to purchase. And if you've bought a shampoo for a specific purpose, you can select a moisturizing conditioner that will enhance that purpose as well.

However, the benefits of all this depend greatly on how amenable your cat is to bathing! If grooming is a struggle, an all-in-one product containing shampoo, moisturizer, and conditioner will make the routine less time consuming and thus less stressful. However, you will probably obtain better results by applying a leave-on moisturizer and conditioner after the initial shampooing. There are also excellent moisturizing and conditioner sprays that can be spritzed on once the coat has dried.

FACIAL CLEANSERS

The best beauty routine may well require the use of a variety of products. For example, if you need to treat a problem like a skin allergy, use a specially formulated product on the body and a different, gentler feline shampoo for the facial area. There are also specially flavored feline facial masks designed to cleanse the sensitive facial area. If you get the product on your cat's nose or lower lip, she can lick it off quite harmlessly and even enjoy the flavor! And it will not irritate the eyes.

CATS AND WATER: TURNING BATH TIME INTO A SENSUAL FELINE EXPERIENCE

The general perception is that cats hate water, but in fact, they are natural swimmers. Certain breeds such as Abyssinians and Turkish Vans may even willingly join you in the shower! This misconception probably persists because the average domestic feline isn't usually exposed to water on a regular basis. Most cats only get to dip their paws under a running faucet or into that glass of water you've put on the bedroom nightstand to drink during the night. Consequently, if you suddenly fling your fur kid into the tub, she's going to resist and protest loudly. But if you introduce her to water from kittenhood, she will learn to tolerate a bath—and may even enjoy it.

Unless you have a show cat who needs to be fur-fabulous for the show ring, she can probably be bathed every few months and cleaned in between with specially formulated wipes and mousses. There's no standard routine—do what works best for you and your fur kid.

CREATING THE RIGHT ENVIRONMENT

You can turn bath time into a pleasant and sensual experience for both you and your kitty by burning some specially formulated pet aromatherapy candles.

If you introduce your feline to water from kittenhood, she will learn to tolerate a bath—and may even enjoy it. Fill the sink with only enough lukewarm water to wet her fur, shampoo, rinse, and dry off with a fluffy towel.

They will have a calming effect, absorb that wet fur smell, and generally set the mood for a relaxing time. Before you begin, you can also spray a feline pheromone product into the bathroom to promote a sense of calm and well-being. And don't laugh—a little soothing music will also help turn bath time into an enjoyable ritual.

Most importantly, you have to listen to your cat, especially if you have adopted an older individual who possibly has never been bathed before. Lots of soulful meowing is a stress indicator. The experience could get her heart to race and her sugar levels to spike dramatically. If you think that a bath may be too much of an ordeal, resort to using waterless products. (See "Bath Plan B.")

PREPARING FOR BATH TIME

It's a good idea to get everything ready before you bring your cat into the equation, and that includes removing any knots in her fur beforehand. If you are going to use pet aromatherapy candles, light them half an hour in advance.

It's a good idea to have everything ready before bringing your cat to her bath.

Make sure that you have your shampoo and conditioning products open and have at least two towels in place. Special absorbent pet towels are excellent for removing excess water before you wrap your fur ball in an ordinary towel. If possible, warm your towels in advance by placing them in the dryer.

Remember, you have options. You can bathe kitty in a deep sink, in your bathtub, or even in the shower stall. It will depend on how tolerant she is. Wherever you decide, be sure to put down a rubber mat or a towel on which she can stand. This will give her traction and make bath time less stressful for her—and for you.

Often, cats don't like the sound of handheld shower sprays more than the actual water. The best way to deal with this type of hesitant cat is to place her in position and have several buckets of warm water on hand along with a sponge and a cup. The idea is to use the first bucket of water to sponge her before and during the shampooing and conditioning ritual and then to use the second bucket of water and cup to gently pour water over her fur for the final rinse.

THE ACTUAL BATH

Start washing your cat from her neck down to her toes and tail. Massage the bath formula into her fur—she will like that part. Dab shampoo and conditioner onto a cotton ball, and work gently around the eyes, nose, and ears and under the chin. Some cats may prefer the use of a pet wipe on

Spray-on or mousse shampoos work best on water-phobic cats.

the facial area or even a facecloth with ordinary warm water. If you use a specially formulated facial mask, you can apply it and remove it before you place your cat in the bath. This type of product has the added bonus of lightening any brown stains below the eyes and along the side of the nose area on pale-furred felines.

If you are using any kind of special skin treatment, experts suggest that you apply it twice during a bath for it to effectively treat the condition. Leave the second application on for 5 to 15 minutes (kitty permitting, of course!) to allow the active ingredients to be properly absorbed.

Rinse the fur well to remove all traces of shampoo and conditioner, especially if you are using the "buckets-of-water" routine. If you are showering the products off, allow the water to run over your cat for at least five minutes to enable her skin to be properly hydrated. It's very important to rinse well because products that are not designed to be left on can cause irritation. They may also be ingested when your cat takes over her own grooming and starts licking herself after you've completed the bath. Also, never allow water to enter your cat's ears—fold them over when rinsing. It's not a good idea to place cotton balls in the ears because you may forget to remove them.

When your fur kid is thoroughly rinsed and while she is still in the tub, use an absorbent pet towel to remove excess water. Then scoop her up in a warm, dry, fluffy one for the final toweling.

Longhaired cats should be gently brushed or combed after a bath so that their fur doesn't mat during the drying process. If you are going to use a hair dryer, make sure that it's made specifically for pets because those designed for humans are far too hot.

No matter how efficient you are and how wonderful the experience is, you will probably still get a look from your cat that implies you didn't do a proper job, so she is now forced to "clean up" after you! But that's just her natural instinct—it's what cats do.

BATH PLAN B: WATERLESS SPRAY-ON AND MOUSSE PRODUCTS

Apart from a typical bath routine, there are many other viable bathing options. Waterless spray-on or mousse products are formulated with water-phobic felines in mind. They work efficiently to keep fur fabulous, and as a result, "bath time" instantly becomes a less stressful experience. These products are also easy to use when you simply want to do a quick "top and tail" cleanup in a hurry or want to remove a single dirty spot.

USING WATERLESS PRODUCTS

Waterless spray-on products and mousses work on the water and paper towel principle. They all contain a diluted form of shampoo that is effective enough to clean but not strong enough to leave any residue on the skin or hair. The key to success depends on the manner in which they are applied.

For a very dirty coat, first spray your pet with a fine mist of warm water or wet the coat with a strong paper towel. You can also use absorbent, sponge-type towels found in the household cleaning supplies aisle at the supermarket.

Spray the product directly onto your hands. If you are using a mousse, fill the palm of your hand liberally with the foam. Use two fingers to apply it directly to your cat's body, starting at the neck and working down the body and legs. Next, rub the product in with a warm, wet, squeezed-out washcloth, working all the way down to the skin. Rinse the cloth often, and keep wiping until there is no more mousse left on the hair. You can repeat this procedure as many times as is necessary—or as long as your pet will allow!

Dry the coat with a paper towel, and immediately get to work with a brush or comb.

If the coat just needs freshening in between regular grooming, simply apply the product, massage it into the coat, rub with a soft towel, and brush afterward.

To clean the facial area, place some product in a saucer and dip a cotton swab or cotton ball into it. Apply it carefully to the areas around the nose, eyes, and mouth. Wipe it off with a tissue or soft towel.

Some mousse products have a comb attachment that fits directly into the container, which really makes the application quicker and more efficient.

WET WIPES AND CLEANSING CLOTHS

When using wipes or cleansing cloths, only use products specially formulated for cats. Standard wipes contain alcohol, which is extremely drying to feline skin and fur. They can also interfere with the pH balance of your pet's skin and may cause irritations.

Specially formulated premoistened wipes are great for grooming elderly kitties who are no longer capable of doing an efficient job themselves. Look for products that clearly state that they are "lick safe" and "nontoxic" on the label, and look for ingredients such as vitamin E and aloe.

Keep It Down!

Hairdryers and vacuum cleaners rank #1 on your cat's top-ten list of things she hates because the noise is very irritating to her sensitive ears—cats can hear at frequencies of 50 to 60 kHz, while humans only hear 18 to 20 kHz. Be sure to purchase a special pet dryer that is low in noise and has heat settings designed for safe use on feline skin and fur. If your cat tends to wriggle a lot, consider purchasing a pet dryer on a stand so that you can use both hands to dry her more efficiently.

Grooming: Longhaired Versus Shorthaired Cats

For longhaired breeds, double-sided wire and bristle brushes are useful, and slicker brushes and wide-toothed combs help long hair remain mat- and tangle-free.

For shorthaired cats, your basic toolkit should include a bristle brush, a rubber curry brush, a flea comb, and a chamois.

Regardless of fur length, if your fur kid's coat is in tip-top condition, she will enjoy a massage with a "zoom groom" long-toothed rubber massage brush. It has bigger teeth than a curry brush.

DON'T GIVE YOUR CAT THE BRUSH-OFF

Although you may only bathe your fur kid occasionally, don't give her the brush-off just because she appears to handle grooming herself quite well on her own. Regular proper brushing and combing not only remove dead fur and control shedding but will also help distribute the natural oils in the skin, which are needed for a shiny and healthy coat. If you ask professional groomers the secret to their success, they'll tell you that it has a lot to do with the tools of their trade combined, of course, with their expertise in using them.

One of the best ways to learn about grooming tools is to page through mail-order catalogs or browse online. Once you have gained some general knowledge, it's a good idea to research them further at a store so that you can actually get to handle the tools you are interested in buying.

If you have a pedigreed kitten or cat, you can seek grooming advice from the breeder. He will also be able to give you hands-on knowledge regarding the best tools pertaining to your breed's fur type.

Although people often think that cats automatically enjoy being brushed, this is not always the case. Many will squirm around and even try to bite your hand to distract you and get you to stop. Once again, if you introduce a beauty routine from kittenhood, your cat should learn to enjoy being pampered with a brush. However, cats can be very selective about the grooming tools they will tolerate, so you are going to have to experiment.

GROOMING TOOLKIT BASICS

A basic grooming toolkit for your fur kid should include the following:

- **Slicker brush.** A cheap and inexpensive slicker brush removes tangles, dead hair, and debris while distributing healthy coat oils.
- **Nylon brushes.** Using a selection of brushes with nylon bristles gives the coat a smooth and silky look.
- **Short-toothed comb.** A fine, short-toothed comb gently removes any matted hair from

the fur as well as hair from the slicker brush.

- ✤ **Deshedding comb.** A deshedding comb helps keep the undercoat thinned without cutting the hair.

- ✤ **Flea comb.** A fine-toothed flea comb removes both fleas and eggs from the fur and also gently grooms facial areas.

- ✤ **Hair mitt.** A hair-grabbing mitt removes loose hair and also offers a nice back massage at the same time.

- ✤ **Rubber comb.** A rubber comb with large teeth, also known as a curry brush, magnetically lifts fur and massages the skin.

- ✤ **Massage roller brush.** With the trend toward pet lifestyle products that mimic human products, an item such as a massage brush that spins away loose hair and massages simultaneously is something your cat may enjoy immensely. The rubber bristles are ergonomically designed to gently remove loose dead hair, dried dirt, and dander while providing a soothing body massage. Most models on the market have two speeds and a motor that's silent, so it won't alarm your feline.

- ✤ **Nail clippers and nail files.** There's a variety of nail clippers on the market. The latest hi-tech nail trimmers come with a built-in light so that it's easy to see where to cut. Some even have a light indicator that turns green when you are at the right place to clip. They are a worthwhile investment because a cat's nails can grow quickly, especially on the front paws.

- ✤ **A hairdryer.** If you asked your cat, she'd tell you that noisy hairdryers rank alongside vacuum cleaners as one of the noises she hates most. Human hairdryers are usually far too hot and will burn your pet's sensitive skin, even on the lowest heat setting. Specially designed pet dryers have heat settings that are tolerable to pet skin and hair, and they are relatively low-noise. The best investment is to buy a

Brushing and combing not only remove dead fur and control shedding but will also help distribute the natural oils in the skin, which are needed for a shiny and healthy coat.

model that comes with suction feet or a clip-on attachment because it will allow you to use both hands for brushing and drying.

If you are purchasing a new dryer, choose one with the latest ionic technology. Negative ions that exist in the air cause large water droplets on the hair to be broken down into smaller drops. Smaller drops then allow more water to be absorbed into the hair so that it can dry more quickly and simultaneously retain moisture. As a result, fur is smooth and holds less static.

HOW TO BRUSH YOUR CAT

Begin every grooming session by running your hands over your cat's body from head to tail. This is the easiest way to find any mats, which must be removed before you begin brushing all over with long strokes. Gently comb them out with a fine-toothed comb. A light dusting of cornstarch will help loosen the hair and make it easier to detangle. Very tight mats need to be cut out using blunt-tipped scissors. If you have a longhaired breed, check for mats between the toes, in the ears (especially if your cat has "ear curls"), and around the legs and rear. Regular grooming will help keep mats to a minimum.

Once mats are removed, you are ready to begin brushing. Always start in the same place and work your way around your cat's body. This is important if you are going to establish a routine that she will ultimately learn to enjoy. Be patient! Lots of cats don't like being brushed at first but get used to it when they discover that they are spending quality time with their pet parents. If necessary, bribe your fussing feline with her favorite treat.

Begin by brushing your cat's head. Use soft, gentle strokes in the direction in which the fur lies as you work your way down the body, sides, and legs. Cats have sensitive skin, so don't brush hard. If you don't feel that you're getting all the hair off, come back and do a second (or even a third) brushing until you get all the loose fur. Remove the hair from the brush whenever it gets full so that you don't put the loose fur back on your cat.

Apart from spending quality time together, you are also helping your feline out because excess hair swallowed during her own grooming routine causes hairballs and constipation. You will be cutting down on the amount of hair that will be shed around your home, too.

You may have to step up your routine in the spring, when cats begin shedding their winter coats, and again in the fall, when they grow new fur for winter.

GROOMING SCHEDULE

Brushing and combing your cat should never be considered a chore. I like to think of it as spending wonderful quality time together. Nevertheless, it's important to develop good grooming habits from kittenhood or from the moment your fur kid comes into your life.

Grooming sessions will be easier for everyone if you let her pick the spot where she'd like you to groom her. My cat Fudge likes to flop down on the kitchen counter for a brushing session, while my cat Cali loves to be brushed when she's lying in her favorite sun spot on the carpet or when she's snoozing on the bed.

Naturally, longhaired breeds need more grooming than shorthaired breeds, and you need to take this into account when adopting a regular routine. Longhaired cats such as Persians and Himalayans need daily brushing. So do shorthaired breeds with double coats such as the American Shorthair, British,

The benefits of regular grooming sessions go beyond good looks—they will reinforce the bond you share with your feline companion.

Manx, Russian Blue, and Scottish Fold. Those with medium coats such as the Balinese, Javanese, and Turkish Angora can be groomed twice weekly. Other shorthaired cats can be well maintained with a weekly brushing session. Cats with short slick coats such the Siamese and Oriental Shorthair may only need a weekly rubdown with a chamois cloth.

PUTTING ON THE GLITZ: COSMETIC PRODUCTS YOU SHOULDN'T BE WITHOUT

These days there are lots of specially made feline beauty products designed to bring out natural highlights, cover those pesky gray and faded patches, hide brown stains, and add luster and shine to your glamour puss's fur.

HIGHLIGHTS AND COLOR ENHANCERS

After-bath products work best to add natural streaks and glints. For white fur, use spray-on whiteners with blue colorants. These contain optical isomers that pick up light rays and "bend" them to give the effect of highlights, making hair look shiny and whiter.

Mica is another ingredient to look for on a label. It's a natural mineral that also makes white hair look dazzling and sun-kissed. Purple or red mica will add glints to all the darker hair tones ranging from brown to auburn shades and black.

HAIR MASCARA FOR COLOR TOUCHUPS

For special occasions or family photo "pawtraits," you can quite safely apply a water-soluble human hair mascara to touch up the odd bit of gray hair or fading color on your pet's fur. Hair mascaras come in a variety of colors and blend in beautifully with all fur tones. They are available at most beauty supply stores. They brush out and of course wash out easily. However, it's not advisable to use them on a fur spot that your cat can easily lick.

To apply the mascara, part the fur with your fingers and apply it evenly using small brush strokes. It's not necessary to go all the way down to skin level. It's the cosmetic visual effect that counts.

CHALK CONCEALER BEAUTY STICKS

Special pet chalk products are great for touching up fading hair color spots and concealing gray. For cosmetic touch-ups, special white pet chalk works particularly well to conceal brown stains on facial fur around the eyes and lower jaw.

Chalk is available in a spray-on formula and also in block form. It comes in basic colors: white, auburn, medium brown, and black. These products are easy to use and are best applied with a soft toothbrush. They also wash out with a quick shampoo. Be sure to check the label to ensure you are purchasing a product for cats.

TEARSTAIN REMOVERS

There are several product formulas on the market designed to cover up and even fade brown tearstains and facial fur discolorations. Many come with special tool applicators. Always be sure to read the instructions carefully. These products are readily available from high-end pet boutique and from on-line stores.

PUMP UP THE VOLUME FOR BIG HAIR DAYS

If you're looking to create a fun effect, you can quite safely borrow a soft hair mousse or fine hairspray from your own beauty shelf and use them on your cat. Both work well to hold spiky, funky looks in place and can be used with most fur types.

Work mousse in with your fingers. Never spray hairspray directly on your cat; instead spritz a small amount onto a brush or comb, or spray it on your fingertips and work it into the ends of the coat.

There are also specially formulated pet products to fluff up and glamorize fur. It's worth investing in a bottle because these can also be used at any time as a grooming aid. They are usually available from on-line specialist grooming stores.

Grooming the Older Cat

If you have a senior cat, you may have to groom her every day. As cats age, they lose flexibility in their muscles and joints and may not be able to bend, stretch, and reach to wash themselves like they used to. This is why they often look unkempt or scraggly. Older cats also may lose interest in their appearance and won't wash as often as they once did.

You can help to keep your older cat looking great by gently brushing (or combing) her each day. Brushing helps to spread natural oils on the fur and prevents it from becoming dry and frazzled looking. It also increases blood circulation and stimulates the nervous system, which makes your cat feel good.

Be gentle and don't rush when you're grooming your older cat. Take things slow and easy, and stop if she becomes upset, anxious, or scared. With the right amount of patience and love, you can keep your senior cat looking great for the rest of her life.

Chapter Two

Healthy Skin

There's a reason why cats wear the sobriquet "glamour puss" with such style and aplomb: Felines always look fabulous. It's estimated that they spend about 10 percent of their waking hours grooming themselves. But there's a more practical reason that they manage to look so elegant and lustrous—they don't suffer from nearly as many skin afflictions as dogs do. However, although cats are rather efficient self-cleaning creatures, they do need our help from time to time to rid them of conditions that may make their skin look and feel less than lovely.

Aside from basic good care and grooming, learning to recognize feline skin problems is also a crucial step in maintaining a healthy skin care regimen. And there are very simple guidelines to help you make basic, nonveterinary diagnoses so that you can make better choices for your fur kid. For example, redness on the skin is an indication of a superficial skin problem that may be caused by an allergic reaction to a variety of things in her environment, such as pollen, grass, a particular food, too much sun, and of course, fleas. It may even be a contact allergy to common household cleaning products. On the other hand, dry, flaky skin or excessively oily skin are often warning signals alerting you to the fact that there could be a serious internal problem, such as diabetes, liver disease, or a kidney problem, all of which require proper veterinary diagnosis and attention.

Up-to-date cat owners know that good grooming is necessary for optimal health and well-being, but they also know that some problems require professional help. Let's look at the various issues that may make your fur kid scratch that itch or send her to the vet.

SKIN ALLERGIES

Allergies are common in cats. Symptoms occur because the animal's immune system is hypersensitive to foreign substances. These sensitivities are often expressed by itchy skin in one spot or all over the body. But as already mentioned, there are many factors that may cause problematic skin. You're going to have to play detective to find out what is causing your fur kid grief. It's called "The Elimination Game."

FLEA-BITE ALLERGIES

Looking for fleas is probably a good place to start. These pesky parasites can hop on any pet or person coming into your home and then transfer to your feline's soft, warm fur, where they will freeload and multiply until you forcefully evict them. Regularly inspect your cat's fur carefully, and take action the moment you spot a single flea. While most cats can handle fleabites well enough, just one bite can result in severe itching that causes some to chew and bite at their skin so ferociously that sores and bacterial infections develop. If this is the case with your fur kid, visit the vet, who can put her on a monthly flea preventive, or in extreme cases, can give her steroid injections.

INHALANT ALLERGIES

Surprisingly, inhalant allergy is the most common of all feline allergies. And most cats won't react to it by sneezing but rather by intensely scratching themselves. Many inhalant allergies tend to be seasonal, but some cats may be allergic to several allergens and could suffer year-round discomfort. Major culprits include pollens, grasses, molds, mildew, and dust mites.

Your best bet is to keep an allergy-sensitive cat indoors; cats are always safer if they enjoy an indoor lifestyle anyway. However, if your pet does have access to a secure outdoor area, it may be advisable to keep her inside during allergy season, when the pollen count is high. Keep her inside when the lawn is being mowed as well.

You may also have to brush up on your housecleaning skills to keep dust mites to a minimum. There are fantastic new vacuum cleaners on the market that incorporate ultraviolet light technology; these work by deactivating the DNA of dust mites, flea eggs, and other bacteria, thus destroying their ability to multiply. Whoever thought a vacuum cleaner could be your fur kid's new best friend?

Even though cats are rather efficient self-cleaning creatures, they do need our help from time to time to keep their skin in top condition.

FOOD ALLERGIES

It's estimated that 10 to 20 percent of feline allergies are food related. Cats have been known to develop an allergic reaction to foods, even after they've been eating them for an extended period. Aside from itching, food allergies are often accompanied by other symptoms, such as wheezing, diarrhea, and vomiting, which will help with your detective work in finding the culprit to her skin problems. Don't overlook checking out her favorite treats, too.

Play the elimination game by stopping her treats first. If the problem persists, seek advice from your vet. He may want to test her for food allergies by putting her on a special hypoallergenic diet.

There's also a possibility that it's not what's in the bowl but the bowl itself that is causing the problem. Many veterinarians believe that plastic food and water bowls can exacerbate skin conditions such as feline acne. There is no absolute proof that cats can be allergic to plasticware, but it's worth upgrading from plastic to glass, ceramic, or stainless steel bowls as a precautionary measure. Apart from blending well with the interior design of your home, these materials are definitely easier to keep clean.

CONTACT ALLERGIES

Contact allergies are the least common allergies in cats, but they are worth investigating. They result from an overreaction to a substance to which your cat's skin is exposed, such as certain plants, topical medications, wool blankets, flea collars, etc. A product you're using to clean carpeting or flooring could be a problem, too. Remember, your fur kid walks and snoozes directly on these surfaces and consequently has direct skin contact with various household cleaning products. Or perhaps the detergent you are using to wash your kitty's favorite blanket or her stuffed toys is the cause.

Feline Dermatitis

In both humans and animals, "dermatitis" is the general term used to denote a condition that causes the skin to be inflamed. However, never treat your cat's rashes, lumps, or bumps with human topical creams and medications because they are too strong for feline skin.

Sometimes the symptoms take time to develop, so you may have to do some careful sleuthing to search out these potential irritants. Once you determine what the culprit is, removing it will usually get rid of the allergy.

UNIDENTIFIABLE ALLERGIES

It's certainly worth trying to resolve the cause of the skin allergy that is afflicting your fur kid yourself, but if your detective work doesn't yield any concrete evidence, you may have to take a trip to the vet for allergy tests. He will diagnose the problem and possibly give your cat some antihistamines.

FELINE ACNE

Do cats actually get acne? Yes, they most certainly do! Unfortunately, unlike with human teenagers, their bad skin isn't linked to hormonal changes and can afflict them throughout their life. Furthermore, feline acne doesn't discriminate between genders and affects both queens and toms equally. However, pet parents are lucky in that their fur kids don't go around slamming doors and bemoaning their bad skin, claiming that they're too ugly to be seen in public. They simply get on with being feline, which means that you are the one who has to attend to their acne problems.

Just like in humans, the blackheads that emerge are the result of oily, blocked skin pores. In felines, this skin disorder manifests itself on the

Aside from basic good care and grooming, learning to recognize feline skin problems is also a crucial step in maintaining a healthy skin care regimen.

chin and around the edges of the lips. Naturally, it's more noticeable on white and light-furred felines. Because cats tend to scratch to soothe irritation, the area can become infected, causing the blackheads to turn into pussy pimples.

Even though feline acne doesn't look very nice, it's best to leave it alone, especially if it isn't bothering your cat. But the moment she starts scratching and the area appears swollen, get the travel carrier out and prepare for a trip to the vet.

Feline acne can be treated and resolved by a vet with prescribed topical medications, or if necessary, antibiotics. Never try to treat the condition with over-the-counter human acne remedies because they are too strong for feline skin and will burn the very sensitive facial area. Clipping the facial hair around affected areas will allow topical treatments to work more effectively, and a daily wash using a cotton ball soaked in a solution of Epsom salts will help keep the area clean.

LUMPS AND BUMPS

Cats don't get moles like people do. However, they do get lumps. These can be as innocuous as a sebaceous cyst, which is a small sac containing an accumulation of secretions from the sebaceous glands in the skin, or they can also be a tumor.

If you notice a suspicious lump or bump on your cat's body, take her to the vet. It's important to determine that any growth you find isn't cancerous by having it surgically removed and sent for a biopsy. If it turns out to be a sebaceous cyst, that will be the end of the story and no further treatment will be necessary. However, if it's a malignant growth and tests indicate that it shows the early stages of cancer, this is one of the few opportunities for which surgical removal can be curative.

It's worth noting that cats can develop lumps for a number of other reasons, too. An infected cat bite can turn into an abscess. A lump can also be the result of a knock or some other kind of trauma. Whatever the cause, have it checked out right away to provide the best possible outcome.

LENTIGO: BEAUTY SPOTS

Although cats don't get age-related moles, orange cats can suffer from an age-related pigment change that appears as a black spot on the lip, the nose, or the eyelid. Called lentigo, these spots are totally harmless. Your cat doesn't have to be completely orange to get one of them, either—even a small tuft of orange fur on her body will be enough for her to get one of these "beauty spots." And don't think that you're dreaming if one day you look at her and the spot seems to have moved or disappeared. That's what they do!

HOT SPOTS

Cats don't suffer from hot spots the way dogs do. Any red spots, especially those on the head or around the tail, are usually signs of something else, such as a condition called feline miliary dermatitis. The word "miliary" actually refers to millet seeds, which these itchy lesions resemble. This condition is also known as feline eczema. It could be caused by an allergy, or it could be a secondary symptom for some other problem, such as stress or separation anxiety. Once again, don't take chances—seek professional advice.

DRY SKIN

Cats can get dry skin, just as humans can. They need to drink lots of water to keep their skin well hydrated, especially if their diet consists of dry food. Ah! This brings us to the water debate: Is bottled water better for your cat than the kind you get from the tap? Simply, the answer lies in doing for her what you do for yourself. If you drink tap water, then fill pet bowls accordingly. If you use a filter or purifying system in your home, let your feline drink from that source. If your cat suffers from urinary tract crystals, distilled water is probably the best water source because it has no impurities; veterinarians often recommend it for this reason.

INCREASING WATER INTAKE

Different cats have different drinking habits. Some love to drink running water, while others like to lap it up from a bowl. You can cater to all feline quirks by installing a pet water fountain. They come with a filter that will remove impurities from the water and give your cat the choice of drinking flowing or still water.

To my knowledge, no study exists to determine what type of water supply cats enjoy most, but pet parents have often told me that if their pet enjoys a particular water source in the home, they tend to drink more. My cat Cali loves to drink out of a glass and somehow always manages to get to the one I put on the nightstand before I do! To combat the problem, I invested in glass water flutes especially designed for pets. I've done my own in-house tests by putting down both an ordinary bowl and the water flute, and Cali automatically gravitates to the flute. She also loves to drink the flowing fountain

If not well hydrated, cats can get dry, itchy skin just as humans can.

33

water. My other feline, Fudge, isn't interested in the fountain, but she loves the water flutes and will drink from them over a standard water bowl any time.

Of course, if you use a pet fountain, regular maintenance is a must. Remember to change the carbon filters at least every six weeks. Put a note on the refrigerator to remind yourself if necessary. Also, if your cat is nervous and easily distracted by household noises, adding a holistic calmative such as Rescue Remedy to the water will help her relax. It's tasteless—and the same remedy works for people, too.

SUN DAMAGE

You know what they say—you can tell the heat of the day by the length of a sleeping cat. It's very true. When cats are hot, they tend to stretch out. But that doesn't mean that they will automatically try to find a cool place in which to sprawl out. In fact, the opposite often applies because they prowl from room to room deliberately seeking out a sunny place, declaring it the perfect snooze zone. This never ceases to amaze me, especially because their basal body temperature is higher than a human's in the first place. Go figure! Yet we are all well aware of the damage the sun's rays can do, and it's an undeniable fact that they can be harmful to pets, too. And don't forget that cats who have an indoor-only lifestyle are still susceptible to sun damage because the sun's harmful rays can penetrate glass.

SUNSCREENS

A cat who lies in the sun too long can get sunburned (solar dermatosis) on the delicate hairless areas of her body, namely the nose, ears, and any pink spots on her tummy that have less hair. She can even suffer sunburn on the pads of her paws, especially if they are pink.

Cats who have dark noses and darker pigment inside their ears are less likely to suffer sun damage. White cats and those with pink noses and ears are the most susceptible. All cats who sunbathe on a regular basis should use a special pet sunscreen, however, so be a good pet parent and monitor your feline's sunbathing routine and apply lotions accordingly.

Choose a product with a minimum SPF 15 protection factor. A lotion with an SPF 30 or SPF 40 is even better. Also, look for products that contain zinc oxide, which is a natural blocking agent that offers effective protection against both UVB and UVA radiation. Read the label carefully to ensure that the product is safe for cats, too, as they tend to lick it off their noses and manage to remove it from their ears as part of their self-cleaning routine. Whatever has been absorbed into the skin will still provide adequate protection, though. Simply apply it more often if necessary.

The areas that need the most protection are the inside tip of the ears, the nose, and any pink areas on the tummy. If you are going to apply it to paw pads, don't use a greasy formula that will

Preventing Sunburn

You may not realize it, but your furry feline friend can suffer from sunburn—even in the house! A cat who lies in the sun too long can get sunburned on the delicate hairless areas of her body, namely the nose, ears, and any pink spots on her tummy that have less hair. She can even suffer sunburn on the pads of her paws, especially if they are pink.

To prevent sunburn, limit the amount of time your cat spends in a safe outdoor enclosure on sunny days, and monitor the amount of time she spends sitting in those warm, sunny spots indoors. The sun's UV rays are strongest between ten o'clock in the morning and four o'clock in the afternoon.

The types of sunburn your cat can get are similar to what humans suffer. They are divided into three levels of severity:

* First degree: The top layer of skin is burned by overexposure to the sun. The skin is pink or red in appearance.

* Second degree: The burn is deeper in that it not only affects the top layer of skin but may also affect other layers. The sunburned skin is red in color, and there may be blisters.

* Third degree: The sunburn affects all the layers of a cat's skin. The skin on the ears and nose may look white. It may even look dried and crusty.

As always, contact your veterinarian if you're not sure whether your cat is sunburned.

leave tracks on your carpets. For hairless breeds like the Sphinx, it may be a good idea to get your cat used to wearing a lightweight T-shirt to better protect her body from damaging rays.

HARMFUL EXPOSURE

As with humans, the biggest problem concerning excessive sun exposure is that it can lead to skin cancer, which is especially common in cats with pink skin and white fur. What can appear to be a harmless scratch on the face, particularly on the nose and ears, could be the start of solar-induced squamous cell carcinoma. Crusty sores on the tips of the ears, the lips, and the nostrils may also indicate skin cancer. Often, affected areas are itchy, and scratching tends to make the skin even more red and inflamed.

Veterinary evaluation is necessary if you find any spots or lesions that seem suspect. But sadly, by the time medical intervention is usually sought, it's often too late and the cancer literally eats away the affected areas. Treated in its early stages, squamous cell carcinoma can be cured.

SUNBATHING ALTERNATIVES

If you are worried that your cat's coloring could predispose her to skin cancer, try offering her some satisfying alternatives.

A cat who lies in the sun too long—even indoors—can get sunburned on the delicate hairless areas of her body, namely the nose, ears, and any pink spots on her tummy that have less hair.

Thermal Cushions and Blankets

Try to control your cat's sunbathing habits by placing bubble wrap on her favorite sun spot, which will force her to go elsewhere. Elderly cats in particular enjoy the warmth of the sun, so instead of allowing kitty to sunbathe, provide her with a thermal cushion or blanket as a warm and cozy substitute. Place it in her regular sun spot and then slowly move it out of the sun. Hopefully, she won't notice that you've marginally changed her location.

Sun Beds for Cats

Sun beds offer cats another safe alternative to sunbathing. The pet version is a medically designed piece of equipment that provides the same far infrared radiant (FIR) heat as that emitted by the sun but without the damaging ultraviolet rays that cause the skin to burn. Naturally, this "sun bed" is not designed to give kitty a tan but instead offers deep-penetrating, healing warmth, which is also excellent for aching joints and muscles. It can even help alleviate skin problems and is beneficial in promoting quick healing of the skin after surgery.

So if your cat is a sun seeker, and particularly if she's elderly and a little arthritic, you can give her the same therapeutic relief the warmth of the sun offers by investing in a pet sun bed instead.

Tattoos

Because cats who have darker pigmentation on their nose and inner ears are less likely to suffer from sunburn, veterinarians have been known to suggest tattooing a pink nose black. This is a drastic remedy to ensure that the sun's rays won't cause damage to this rather delicate and highly susceptible area. The tattoo has to be done under anesthesia by a veterinarian or a professional tattoo artist.

But just as deciding to have any type of corrective or plastic surgery is a major decision for humans, the same amount of thought should go into making a similar decision for your cat. By changing her nose from pink to black, you are essentially changing her looks—and possibly your perception of her personality. This is a drastic measure, so think twice.

Never Bald, Forever Beautiful

Cats are lucky because they never show their age with thinning hair or baldness; new hairs constantly grow alongside old hairs. However, if your fur kid develops an itch from a fleabite or as the result of some kind of irritant or allergy, she will begin to scratch and pull hair out in an attempt to relieve the discomfort. If you do not step in and provide permanent relief, the action can become compulsive. Obsessive-compulsive disorders are quite common as a result, and even if the itch is eventually eradicated, some cats continue to overgroom themselves by removing chunks of their fur.

It's important to watch out for signs of constant scratching, particularly in a multi-cat household where a single flea can cause chaos and set off a feline chain reaction. Take notice if your fur kid is scratching continually—this is a feline cry for help.

OUTDOOR SKIN IRRITANTS: INSECTS

If you have a safe outdoor enclosure that allows your fur kid to enjoy some fresh air, she may be plagued by irritating flies, mosquitoes, and even ants at certain times of the year.

A safe way to deal with these irritants is to use a topical repellant. One of the easiest products to use is a special felt-tipped pen (which resembles a highlighter) containing nontoxic ingredients that will prevent flies and insects from bugging her. They are available from online stores and holistic veterinarians. Simply dab the pen on the inside of your cat's ears, which will keep pests away from her face, and at the base of her tail, preferably on a spot that she will have difficulty reaching to lick, to protect her body.

If your fur kid does have the luxury of lounging in a safe, sunny outdoor environment, make sure that she has plenty of water at her disposal as well as a shady retreat so that she doesn't become dehydrated or sunburned.

Sting Like a Bee

If your cat has been chasing around after a bee and suddenly has a lump on the inside of her cheek that makes her look like a hamster storing grapes, chances are she chomped down on it and her snack stung her in return! It may be difficult to remove the stinger from inside her mouth. In fact, it will probably be impossible to get her to sit still long enough for a proper inspection. A veterinarian-prescribed antihistamine may be the only way to get the swelling to subside. Please don't head for the bathroom shelf and look for medicated relief meant for humans, which is inappropriate and could possibly harm your cat.

STRESS AND SEPARATION ANXIETY

Cats can suffer from stress and anxiety, especially if they are left home alone for extended periods. It's often difficult for pet parents to accept this because felines seem to lead such laid-back lives. But because they are creatures of habit and are very perceptive, changes in their routine can put them out of sync. If your cat develops a bald spot or is pulling out chunks of her fur (psychogenic alopecia), there are other issues at stake as well. Fur pulling can be a secondary response to any number of different stressors. To put it bluntly, Houston, we have a problem. Once again, get that travel carrier out and prepare for takeoff to the vet.

Apart from chewing on or pulling out her fur, if your cat suddenly starts behaving strangely—hiding and refusing to come out or avoiding her litter box—you must find what's causing these behavioral changes. Simple things can have an affect on her behavior. For example, a new baby in the house or a new pet is a common cause of stress, as is moving to a new home. Some cats don't even like it when their parents rearrange the furniture. In extreme cases of fur pulling or any other serious behavioral change that seems prolonged, get professional help.

Climbing on the Couch for a Little Therapy

Lots of wonderful books explain common scenarios that affect feline behavior. If you've already tried everything you know and your cat is still having problems, consider consulting a professional behaviorist.

Keeping your feline's skin healthy will make her feel good all over.

Follow the same advice given to people caring for children: Root out the cause and work through the problem to resolve it. Typical behavioral problems need to be treated seriously because they will affect your feline's life and thus yours. And most can be fixed!

Recently, a Japanese company introduced a patch designed to detect stress levels in felines by monitoring excessive sweat secretions. But honestly, by simply running through a checklist relating to changes in your cat's routine, you may be able to pinpoint something worrying her and discuss it with your veterinarian.

Under dire circumstances, medications similar to Prozac for pets can help get your kitty back on track.

LOOKING AND FEELING GOOD

In addition to making your cat look good, keeping her skin healthy will make her feel good all over. Once again, take advantage of the moments she jumps onto your lap or flops at your feet looking for a pat to inspect her all over. It only takes a few minutes to ensure that your favorite feline is in top condition. Remember, problems that are detected in the early stages stand a much better chance of being cured. Even though cats are famously self-sufficient, especially in the grooming department, your extra attention and occasional help will make your kitty purr in contentment. What could be better?

Chapter Three

The Pawfect Peticure

*B*efore we begin talking about the "pawfect peticure," it's a good idea to know a little bit about your kitty's toes and how she uses her nails. Cats scratch for a variety of reasons: to sharpen their claws, to mark their territory, to reduce stress, and to exercise. Scratching is a completely normal feline behavior. Whether wild or domestic, you can't stop cats from doing it; it's instinctive. They will scratch their claws on anything that feels good, which is why your kitty claws the upholstery on your favorite chair.

Cats have scent glands on the underside of their front paws. As they scratch, they mark a particular item of furniture with their own scent. Naturally, they always choose your favorite chair to claw because they are attracted to it by *your* scent. However, this action also serves a purpose because it helps strip off old claw sheaths to reveal the sharp new ones underneath.

Claw sheaths that aren't removed by scratching your favorite chair are usually removed when your kitty settles down to manicure her feet, which includes a good licking between the toes and nibbling on her nails. Don't you just love the way cats stop to admire their handiwork when they're done?

Nevertheless, apart from training your cat not to claw your furniture (yes, it can be done), you can control scratching by giving her regular pedicures or letting her wear brightly colored nail covers. And please, there is no justification to declaw your cat

Ouch! My Aching Feet

Declawing is actually an amputation of the last joint of your cat's toes. It's an inhumane, drastic measure and a very painful surgery. During the recovery time, cats don't have the luxury of lying in bed and being waited upon; they still have to walk about. Ouch! And without claws, a cat cannot grasp or hold anything or establish proper footing. Fortunately, declawing is outlawed in many countries and needs to be made illegal in every American state, too. With patience, any cat can be trained to only scratch on designated scratching posts. Declawing is not the answer to furniture preservation.

to prevent her from scratching your furniture. Fortunately, more and more cities across America are now joining the rest of the world and making this practice illegal. Remember, it's a drastic operation that amputates the last joint of your cat's toes, and it's very painful and can cause her discomfort for the rest of her life.

I can't stress enough that from the moment that bundle of fur comes into your life, it's wise to get her used to being petted as a forerunner to grooming. When my cats are sleeping, I often take the opportunity to gently massage them, working my way down to their feet and stroking their toes. If you press gently on the paw pads, the toes automatically splay open. This makes it easy to massage the paw pads. If your cat gets used to you touching her toes, she will more than likely allow you to trim her nails without too much fuss and bother.

PET PEDICURE BASICS

The first rule of a successful pedicure is to ensure that you are sitting comfortably with your fur kid on your lap. Once again, if you hold her regularly in this position, she will be less likely to squirm when the nail clippers come out. However, if she is a squirmer, consider getting an assistant to hold her so that you can trim her nails safely.

Some cats are simply not lap cats. If yours isn't one, trim her nails when she is lying down on the floor. Ask your assistant to crouch over her and hold her firmly between his knees. This way, you can either sit or kneel in front of your kitty and more easily handle her feet. Having her gently restrained will also prevent her from wriggling and being injured and you from being scratched. Worst-case scenario or if you are alone, wrap her in a towel and only expose one foot at a time. I call this the "kitty burrito." This way, she won't be able to bring her back feet around to kick and scratch.

ONE, TWO, THREE—TRIM

To begin your cat's pedicure, pick up a paw and massage the pads. Then press gently so that she spreads her toes and extends her nails. The best way to decide where to cut is to look at the nail from the side, which makes it easier to distinguish between the nail and the quick (the blood

All cats are compelled to scratch as part of their natural behavior.
They scratch to sharpen their claws, to mark territory, and to exercise.

Southpaw

Is your fur kid left-pawed or right-pawed? A study on feline paw preference conducted by Oxford University in England concluded that most cats consistently use their left paws. This led researchers to conclude that cats who favor their left paws (southpaws) are right-brain dominant because it's the right side of the brain that controls movement on the left side of the body and vice versa. Right-brain dominance also means that your "southpaw" is highly intuitive! Other experts believe that felines are ambidextrous.

supply, marked by an opaque pink color at the base of the nail). While trimming, hold the clippers in a vertical position so that the claw is cut vertically instead of horizontally across; this prevents the nail from splitting. Start slowly and only trim one or two nails at a time. As your kitty gets used to the process, you can then extend the grooming routine to include more nails.

Never use human nail cutters because they tend to split the nail, causing lots of rough edges. This is a job that you will be doing regularly, so it's worth investing in a pair of stainless-steel trimmers. If you are worried that you'll cut into the quick, consider buying special clippers that come with a built-in light designed to highlight exactly where to cut the nail. There are also clippers with sensors that light up to indicate the correct cutting zone. Red means don't cut in this area and green means you're safe, so you can clip away comfortably.

If you accidentally clip into the quick, don't panic. Styptic powder will stop the bleeding. Ordinary cake flour will also do the trick. If you don't have special clippers and feel unsure, simply trim the very tips of the nails until you build up more confidence. You can use an ordinary nail file to smooth out any rough edges.

Of course, apart from nail trimmers, the most important "tool" for a pedicure is a packet of treats. The task is undoubtedly done most efficiently when bribery is involved! The idea is for her to munch happily while you clip.

A WORD ABOUT DEWCLAWS

While you are trimming the front paws, be sure to include the dewclaw—the slightly thicker nail on the side of the foot. As with ordinary claws, if the dewclaws are left unattended, they can grow so long that they curl under and grow into the skin. Not only can this be painful, but a bacterial infection may set in. If this happens, you'll need to take your cat to a professional groomer or a veterinarian. On longhaired cats, it may be a good idea to wet the fur in this area to make it easier to see the claw.

After trimming it, dab on a mild antiseptic to keep the area clean.

TRIMMING SCHEDULE

Nails on the front paws grow faster than those on the back paws. After the first two or three grooming sessions, you will be able to gauge how often it's necessary to trim your kitty's claws. Trimming less nail more frequently is better than taking the chance of cutting too deep and hurting your cat. If you cut too deep, it's going to be harder to trim her nails in the future because she will remember what you did on a previous occasion.

NAIL INFECTIONS

Even though cats scratch and claw in a variety of strange places, they do not get nail infections from everyday dirt or household dust. A cat nail fungus called paronychia is more than likely a symptom of some internal problem such as hyperthyroidism, a thyroid condition, or lymphosarcoma, a tumor of the lymphatic tissue rather than a specific infection in the nail bed, both of which require professional intervention.

Use the time you spend on your cat's pedicure to inspect her feet and pads. By regularly inspecting her toes, you will know what they should look like and will be able to gauge if something is amiss that will require further diagnosis by a veterinarian.

Further, always check that nothing is caught between your cat's toes, such as kitty litter. In particular, the sandy clumping type of litter is prone to getting caught between the paw pads, making it uncomfortable for her to walk. Remember, your cat will remove it herself by ingesting it!

ACRYLIC NAILS FOR CATS

Colorful nail covers are a viable alternative to declawing and an excellent way to stop your cat from scratching your favorite chair. Consider them acrylic nails for cats!

Developed by a veterinarian, these nail covers come in various sizes and are applied over the nail with an adhesive. It's a similar procedure to that used in applying acrylic nails for humans. I once asked a veterinarian to apply nail covers to one of my cats, and it was expensive—nearly twice the price of a set of human acrylic nails would cost at a nail salon!

Actually, the procedure is very simple, and you can do it yourself at home. First, trim

After the first few grooming sessions, you will be able to gauge how often it's necessary to trim your kitty's claws.

your cat's claws. Then, apply adhesive into the nail cap and press gently over the claw and hold in place with your thumb and forefinger. The hardest part is trying to get your fur kid to sit still long enough to let the adhesive set.

Once they are put on, chances are kitty will be oblivious to them. They are quite safe, nontoxic, and usually come off with normal shedding. However, don't apply nail covers if your cat is allowed outdoors. A cat's claws are weapons of defense, and your kitty may need to defend herself against predators or other hazards.

Because they are purely cosmetic, you may want to give her a colorful pedicure for a special occasion. There's a wonderful color chart to choose from, including a special selection for the holiday season. So add some glamour, and make your kitty a real Santa Paws at Christmas with bright red and green nails.

Nail covers are sold in a kit form that ostensibly includes a six-month supply. They are available everywhere, from high-end pet boutiques to pet stores and online stores.

OTHER FOOT SAVERS

If you take your cat outdoors during the winter snow season, wipe off her paws with a wet warm towel or paper towel to remove any traces of salt that may be strewn on hard surfaces. The salt and chemicals used to de-ice these areas can be toxic if licked and will irritate soft paw pads.

Also, be wary of antifreeze on driveways. Cats are attracted to its sweet smell and taste. Apart from irritating the skin, it's highly poisonous. Walking on it and licking it off paws afterward can be fatal. An animal poisoned by antifreeze may appear to be intoxicated and have trouble walking and coordinating her movements. If you suspect that your fur kid has ingested antifreeze, don't watch and wait—take her to the vet or animal hospital immediately. Kidney failure can set in within 24 hours.

FOR SCAREDY CAT PARENTS

If you're unsure about how to trim your cat's nails or aren't sure if you should even try, talk to your veterinarian. He can discuss the subject with you and show you how to do it. If you take your cat to a professional pet groomer, a pedicure is included in the service provided. However, if she is using a scratching post on a regular basis, she is probably taking very good care of her own nails the natural way.

Nature's Pedicures

A good scratching post makes a great feline nail file! Apart from keeping claws in check, it also helps keep the front leg and paw muscles toned and healthy. You are going to have to experiment to find out whether your fur kid is a vertical or horizontal scratcher. Some cats like both. Consequently, I have various scratching posts all over the house. It's always a good idea to position them near a favorite nap spot because cats like to stretch and scratch after a good snooze.

When it comes to vertical posts, I like sisal-covered ones the best. They are very durable. Carpeted posts can lead to bad habits because cats often can't distinguish between a carpeted post and the wool carpeting on the floor. Make sure that the post you choose has a nice solid base and is taller than your fur kid, which will allow her to get a good stretch at the same time. There's also a large variety of horizontal scratchers made from recycled corrugated cardboard, which cats seem to love, too.

If you have room in your home for a piece of feline furniture, there are wonderful scratchers shaped like a chaise lounge and other items of furniture made from corrugated cardboard that will give your fur kid both horizontal and vertical scratching options.

The best way to get your cat to try out a new scratching post is to use it yourself! Make sure that your fur kid is watching, and run your fingernails down the post a few times. Chances are she will imitate you and will take over from that moment on. If she's still a bit hesitant, rub a little catnip on the post. That will definitely do the trick.

Chapter Four

Eye Can See Clearly Now

Generally, a cat's eyes require very little attention during grooming. And thank goodness felines don't suffer from nearly as many eye problems as dogs do, because unlike their canine friends, they won't tolerate the indignity of having to wear one of those surgical collars that looks like an inverted lampshade to prevent them from scratching at their eyes.

nd should they require ocular surgery, once again, the chances of them making a public appearance at the veterinarian's office wearing protective dark glasses is probably one in a million! Can't you just see your cat sitting there with an expression on her face that says "purrplease"?

Simply put, most cats won't tolerate any gadgetry around the neck or face beyond a standard collar. But there's a lot you can do to keep your kitty's eyes healthy, well groomed, and protected. Let's take a look.

GENERAL EYE CARE

The best thing you can do for your fur kid from kittenhood is to clean her face regularly with a warm, wet, soft washcloth, and at the same time, wipe her eyes. By establishing this simple routine, you are ensuring that she will tolerate having drops or ointment put in her eyes without too much fuss should she ever develop any eye problems that require treatment.

Although your cat's eyes require very little attention during grooming, always take a minute to check them. Healthy eyes should be clean, clear, and free of discharge.

KEEPING AN EYE OPEN FOR EYE PROBLEMS

Regular grooming sessions are an opportune time to do a general health check. Always take a minute to check your kitty's eyes to make sure that they are clear, clean, and not runny. Taking note of changes that may indicate a problem can also save your feline pal from unnecessary discomfort or serious problems down the road if conditions go untreated. If you notice anything out of the ordinary and aren't sure what to do, call your vet for advice. The following are the most common feline eye conditions. Some may be harmless, but others could have serious consequences without professional intervention.

TEARSTAINS

While most people know what feline tearstains look like, namely those brown streaks on the inside corners of their eyes running down the bridge of the nose, most never stop to question what causes them. One thing is for sure—they're not caused from crying over spilled milk!

> ## Third Eyelid
>
> Cats have a third eyelid, called the nictitating membrane, which is a thin cover that closes from the side and appears when the cat's eyelid opens. If this membrane remains partially closed, it's a sign that your fur kid is sick and needs to be seen by the vet.

Tearstaining is a harmless, natural process more obvious on cats with light-colored fur. Ask any elementary school science student what happens when an iron compound is mixed with oxygen, and if they were paying attention in class, they'll tell you that oxygen causes the iron to rust. Yes, those red-brown tearstains are caused by rust!

To put it in cat terms, the tear glands continually produce secretions that lubricate the surface of the eye and drain down the tear ducts into the nose and throat. However, some liquid tends to accumulate on the skin of the eyelids. As it evaporates, the natural iron compound found in tears mixes with the oxygen in the air and causes those brown strains on the fur. This is particularly common in Persians because the shape of their eyes doesn't allow the tears to drain effectively.

I like to consider tearstains a natural element of feline beauty, rather like freckles in humans. At the same time, I understand the quest for perfection, particularly if your feline is pursuing a career in the show ring. There are numerous products on the market that claim to eliminate tearstains. Some are food additives and can either be sprinkled on food or added to the water bowl. Others are packaged as moistened eye pads that can be used directly on the affected areas. Such products are available from pet boutiques and online stores. It's a good idea to read about them online and compare the various formulations. They do seem to work, but it may be a question of using them permanently. Because the eye area is a delicate one, it's a good idea to get the green light from your veterinarian before trying products on your fur kid.

RED EYES

As with humans, red eyes are a red flag that something is wrong and that your fur kid is going to need your help in determining the cause. Generally, redness is a nonspecific sign of inflammation or infection. It may affect one or both eyes, depending on the cause of the problem. Pay close attention if your fur kid appears to be pawing or rubbing her eyes, squinting, or keeping an eye closed. If symptoms persist or worsen, take your cat to the vet and be sure to tell him about all the signs you've observed.

Tearstaining is a harmless, natural process more obvious on cats with light-colored fur. However, redness or swelling may indicate an infection that requires veterinary care.

FELINE CONJUNCTIVITIS

Although felines don't suffer from a broad spectrum of eye ailments, feline conjunctivitis is very common. It usually starts off as an upper respiratory infection caused by the feline herpesvirus type 1 (FHV-1). The virus is ubiquitous in the cat world. In fact, ophthalmic veterinarians categorically state that every cat on the planet has been exposed to it. Often, it passes from a mother cat to her kittens during the birthing process.

Kittens commonly go through a period of having runny eyes. It's like kids having runny noses. Eventually, their immune system begins to fight back and prevents this type of infection from becoming an ongoing problem. In fact, a cat with a competent immune system is able to generate her own antibodies within seven to ten days. Should the condition linger, however, it can become a problem when it gets into the cornea because it can cause it to ulcerate. And if not treated quickly, your cat can lose sight in the affected eye.

On a positive note, if caught in the early stages, ophthalmic veterinary surgeons can repair the damage by grafting tissue adjunct to the eye onto the cornea. Because the cornea itself doesn't have any blood vessels of its own, by introducing blood vessels that exist in the grafted tissue, the cornea will begin to heal quickly and sight will be restored.

Feline herpesvirus is exclusive to cats and can't be transferred to people. However, like the human herpesvirus, which can cause recurrent cold sores in humans, FHV-1 can remain dormant in felines and flare up at any time. Its reoccurrence is usually stress induced.

GLAUCOMA

Glaucoma is a disease that affects the optic nerve. If left untreated, it can cause blindness. Pressure builds up within the eye, causing engorgement of the deep blood vessels around it. If this intraocular pressure is excessive, the eye becomes stretched and enlarged and loss of vision occurs.

Glaucoma has been nicknamed the "sneaky thief of sight" because the loss of vision usually occurs gradually over a lengthy period and is often only recognized in its advanced stages.

A complete ophthalmic examination includes various specialized tests. More than likely, your veterinarian will refer you to a veterinary ophthalmologist for these tests and subsequent treatment with medication or laser surgery.

ANTERIOR UVEITIS

Anterior uveitis is an inflammation of the front or anterior parts of the eye, called the uvea, and it usually affects the iris as well. This is a painful and potentially vision-threatening disease. The protozoal parasite, toxoplasmosis, is one of the most common causes of this disease in cats, as well as such viruses as feline leukemia virus, feline immunodeficiency virus, and feline infectious peritonitis virus. Topical treatments such as drops or ointments will help reduce the pain and inflammation. However, in a situation where glaucoma may also be diagnosed, surgery to remove the eye may be necessary. Once again, because eye diseases are such a specialized field, you will need to consult with a veterinary ophthalmologist.

ENTROPIAN SURGERY: EYE LIFTS FOR CATS

Sometimes, after lying dormant, FHV-1 can reactivate and cause a nasty black-looking scab in the center of the cornea called a feline sequestrum. Once again, this can be successfully treated. But often, once the cornea is healed, additional eye surgery may be required to prevent the eyelid from rolling inward and causing the eyelashes to irritate the delicate cornea. This is known as entropian surgery, and it is akin to a cosmetic eye lift in people.

In Persians and other brachycephalic breeds (cats who have protruding eyes and squashed-looking faces), congenital entropian defects are quite common; the eyelids tend to roll inward at the corners alongside the nose. However, if the cat makes adequate tears, the fine lashes usually do not irritate the cornea and thus no surgical intervention is necessary.

Catfight!

There's a reason why people always cast aspersions about catfights—because if two cats do get into a spat and their claws come out, the results can be quite nasty. Be sure to check your fur kid's eyes if she's been involved in a feline altercation. A laceration to the cornea can develop into an ulcer, which requires urgent medical care.

EYE IMPLANTS

When a cat loses an eye, a veterinarian will usually suture the eyelid shut. Sadly, the result will make your fur kid's face look very lopsided. And as it heals, the area will develop a sunken and pitted appearance. While this will in no way bother your feline, it's cosmetically unattractive.

Should you ever be faced with this situation, ask your veterinarian to immediately refer you to a veterinary ophthalmologist, who can cosmetically implant a silicone ball into the eye socket during the initial eye removal surgery. These days, this operation is very common. The silicone implants are FDA approved, and there are no side effects. The final appearance is definitely worth it.

SUDDEN-ONSET BLINDNESS

Unlike dogs, cats rarely go blind from cataracts developing as a result of old age. However, kidney disease, one of the foremost killers of older cats, can cause sudden blindness. One of the side effects of the disease is high blood pressure, which causes fluids to accumulate beneath the retina. This literally pushes the retina off its anchor points behind the eye, causing a cat to suddenly lose her sight.

Cats are particularly good at masking any loss in eyesight, so once again, it's a matter of keeping a close check and looking for any changes in eye color coupled with strange behavior. When the retina becomes detached, the pupils become permanently dilated and get a yellowish-green sheen. Early detection can result in the situation being successfully reversed.

Elevated blood pressure can be treated with human medications (prescribed by a veterinarian), and ophthalmic veterinary surgeons say that the success rate of retinas reattaching themselves is as high as 75 percent.

LIVING WITH A BLIND CAT

Cats are very adaptable creatures who can overcome the handicap of being blind better than many other animals because they can

Taurine

Taurine is one essential amino acid that all cat foods should include. Cats who do not get enough taurine in their diets can suffer severe eye problems, possibly leading to blindness. It is interesting to note that because canines do not need taurine, it's not usually present in commercial dog foods—so never feed your cat a diet of dog food. It doesn't contain that feline-necessary protein, taurine, or at least not the amount a cat requires for good eyesight and health.

Cat's Eye

Every cat owner can tell you that they have fallen victim to their kitty's long and loving stare—or their look of disdain when they don't approve of something! But in practical terms, aside from amazing vision, a cat's eyes are very large considering the size of her head. They also bulge slightly, providing them with excellent peripheral vision—which is why they never miss a trick. This may explain why they are fond of staring at people. Yet while their unblinking and sometimes unnerving stare may indicate that they are dissatisfied about something, it's just as likely that they're thinking about how wonderful you are. Here's a quick interpretation of what your feline's beautiful eyes may be telling you:

❖ wide open—your cat is alert, curious

❖ half closed—your cat is napping or relaxed and content

❖ pupils dilated— (especially in bright light) your cat is very alert, frightened, or in pain

❖ pupils are narrow slits—your cat is annoyed

❖ staring at you intently—your cat distrusts you or is annoyed

❖ slowly blinking eyes—your cat is relaxed

❖ long slow "blink" directed at you— this is known as a cat "kiss" and is a form of affection

These are all good reasons to make sure that your fur kid's eyes are well taken care of!

The onset of blindness may be difficult to pinpoint because a cat's senses of hearing and smell can often compensate for a decrease in vision.

rely on their other highly tuned senses of smell and hearing. And after all, they are nocturnal!

For example, cats have twice the amount of sniffing surface on the inside of their noses than humans do. They have between 60 and 80 million olfactory cells, while humans have only between 5 and 20 million. So felines definitely have a keener sense of smell than we do. They also have a special scent organ called the Jacobson's organ, located on the palate. It analyzes and literally allows them to taste smells, especially food smells. That's why cats often appear to turn up their noses at particular foods; they are simply giving it the olfactory once-over!

Further, felines have the added advantage of having glands that secrete pheromones on their cheeks, lower legs, and under the tail. So as they rub up against objects, they are in fact leaving a scent trail to give them invisible guidance around the home.

Whiskers also act as kitty radar and are an amazing multi-purpose guidance system. Cats have 24 whiskers arranged in four horizontal rows on either side of the nose. They can move both forward and backward, and the two top rows can move independently of the two bottom rows. In addition to allowing them to gauge if a space is large enough for them to fit through, whiskers also act as current detectors so that the animal can maneuver past objects without touching them. A cat with healthy whiskers is also able to "read" the outline of another animal in the same way a blind person reads Braille.

If your fur kid has lost her sight, it's important to be consistent around the home. Never move the litter box or rearrange the food bowls. And the same goes for rearranging furniture and leaving things lying around the house. Consistency will help your cat feel comfortable and secure. Once a blind cat becomes accustomed to her new world, she can maneuver around the house, often memorizing the location and distances between objects in the home environment. It's the perfect excuse to insist that everyone tidies up after themselves, too.

It's also essential to ensure that your home is properly cat-proofed to prevent her from becoming injured. Check for broken screens on windows and doors, cover sharp edges on items of furniture, and ensure that toilet seats are kept down at all times. And of course, don't let your blind cat wander outside, even if she was formerly an indoor-outdoor cat.

You'll also have to be aware of your own behavior toward your kitty as well. Because she cannot see you approaching her, be careful not to startle her. Talk to her instead, or perhaps use a pleasant sound such a bell when you want to call her or wake her without startling her by suddenly pouncing on her. Never pick up a blind cat and carry her from one place to another, as she may become disoriented. It's also a good idea to state that your pet is blind on her ID tag and be sure to warn all visitors to your home.

You can enrich your blind cat's life with belled toys and plenty of catnip. If you have other cats, they will soon figure out that she is blind and will become amazingly tolerant of her. By using care and discretion, all can certainly live in harmony and enjoy a wonderful life together.

You can enrich your blind cat's life with belled toys and plenty of catnip.

Chapter Five

Licks and Kisses

Quite frankly, the only cat I've ever known to smile and show lots of perfect teeth is the Cheshire Cat in *Alice in Wonderland.* Alice did a lot of complaining during her misadventures, but one thing she never commented on during her encounter with this cat with the famous supercilious grin was that he had bad breath! In fact, neither did the Duchess, who claimed to know a lot about cats and informed Alice that "*all* cats can grin and most of them do."

I would never argue with the Duchess; she was famous for chopping off people's heads! All cat lovers know about tuna breath, the aftereffect from what is undoubtedly the world's most popular feline food. However, this fishy smell is easily distinguishable from halitosis in the same way that people can tell the difference between someone who has been eating garlic and someone who hasn't brushed their teeth in a while. It's a no-brainer.

If your cat has bad breath, don't think that you can solve the problem with a feline breath mint. It's likely to be a lot more serious because that odor is an indicator that there is something wrong in your cat's mouth and possibly internally, too. It's a frightening statistic, but 70 percent of all cats over the age of three suffer from periodontal disease.

Regular inspections of your fur kid's mouth, along with an annual professional teeth cleaning, are without a doubt the most important health care you can give your feline. If you don't look after her mouth, the bacteria will spread internally when she swallows, entering the bloodstream and possibly causing serious illnesses, such as kidney, heart, and liver disease.

HOW IT ALL STARTS

Dental problems start in your cat's mouth the same way they do in yours. By not taking care of your teeth, you develop plaque, which is nothing more than bacteria buildup on the teeth. And if the plaque is not removed, the minerals in saliva combine with the plaque to form tartar. This in turn irritates the gums and causes gingivitis, which makes the gums around the teeth look red and inflamed. And even if you have a dazzling smile, your breath stinks!

But wait—unfortunately, there's more. Once your cat has gingivitis, the inflammation causes the bone around the roots of the teeth to begin to deteriorate. The teeth then become loose and fall out. This stage of deterioration is called periodontal disease, and the damage is irreversible. If still left unchecked, it will become increasingly difficult for your kitty to eat and will possibly set up a chain

Good oral hygiene is an important part of maintaining your cat's overall health.

reaction in that the bacteria will spread internally and can affect the internal organs.

Periodontal disease can start in cats as young as a year old. But here's the good news: It's completely preventable!

CHECKUPS: SAY "AAH"

It's very important to regularly check your cat's mouth by lifting the lips and looking at the gums. They should be nice and pink and firmly attached to the teeth.

While bad breath is a sign that there's trouble, not all cats get it, which makes it doubly important to keep checking.

HOW TO CLEAN YOUR CAT'S TEETH

There's no question about it—cleaning your fur kid's teeth on a daily basis is an extremely difficult task. Your cat may simply refuse to let you put your fingers in her mouth. And although there are myriad dental products on the market for felines, what's the point if your fur kid is not going to allow you to use them?

Because brushing is the most effective way to control plaque, here is some sound and simple advice I learned from Dr. Jan Bellows of Weston, Florida, who is one of a handful of specialist veterinary dentists registered worldwide. His technique doesn't require toothbrushes and feline toothpastes. Instead, he suggests taking a cotton swab dipped in tuna juice (yes!) and rubbing it along your cat's teeth. Because cats like the taste, you stand a good chance of working your way around the mouth. If not, what you don't achieve today you can do tomorrow. Just keep at it! The mere friction of the cotton swab on the teeth is enough to actively reduce plaque buildup. I told you it was simple!

If that idea doesn't appeal to you, there are other options available. You can use special liquid-filled dental swabs, which are a more sophisticated, ready-to-use version of the cotton swab dipped in tuna juice concept for maintaining a clean and healthy mouth. Other products to consider include specially formulated dental gels and sprays that coat the teeth; these create an invisible barrier that prevents the harmful bacteria that cause plaque and tartar from attaching to the teeth. Such products are applied weekly and are definitely an easier alternative than trying to brush your cat's teeth with a pet toothbrush. Also, check with your veterinarian and ask whether he can recommend any products to put in your cat's drinking water to help decrease plaque.

Say Cheese!

A cat has 30 teeth, 16 on the top and 14 on the bottom. Kittens usually lose their baby teeth between two and four months of age. They have all their permanent teeth by the time they are six months old.

OTHER WAYS TO FIGHT PLAQUE

You can further fight plaque and tartar buildup by feeding your cat a veterinary-prescribed dental food formula. You can even mix it in with your fur kid's ordinary food.

And if you are going to give your kitty treats, you may as well give her something that's going to benefit her teeth at the same time. To find out if the treat you are considering will help maintain a healthy mouth, check to see if the product has a seal of approval from the Veterinary Oral Health Council (VOHC). It's called the VOHC Seal. There's a complete list of foods and treats available on their website www.vohc.org, and it's regularly updated.

TOOTHACHE IN CATS

Yes, despite your best efforts, your cat can suffer from a toothache. Apart from periodontal disease, more than 50 percent of felines have at least one feline odontoclastic resorption lesion, or FORL, by the time they are three years old. Like human cavities, they are extremely painful and can cause difficulty eating.

In humans, tooth decay causes the tooth to disintegrate from the outside inward so that the cavity is visible to the dentist. You may even be able to feel it with your tongue. The exact opposite happens in cats. FORLs cause the tooth to decay from the inside outward. Consequently, you won't see the damage until it's very advanced and irreversible, by which time the tooth will have to be extracted. FORLs are said to be even more painful than human toothaches because the decay attacks the nerve. This is why it's important for your fur kid to have her teeth regularly inspected by a professional—even if you are responsible in offering home care.

MOUTH ULCERS AND SWELLING

Feline gingivostomatitis is a viral infection of the mouth and gums that causes swelling and ulcers. It can also be as painful as a bad toothache. Laser technology is the most effective way of treating it because this precision technique removes the excess tissue in the area and simultaneously reduces the pain caused by the swelling.

THE DENTAL CHECKUP AT THE VETERINARIAN

It's very important to take your pet for a dental checkup or for what veterinarians refer to as an oral dental ATP (an oral assessment, treatment, and prevention checkup) at least once a year.

February is Veterinary Dental Month in the United States, and often veterinarians give special discounted prices. By all means take advantage of such offers, but if your fur kid hasn't had her teeth checked in ages and February is a long way off, please don't wait! It's going to cost you far more if she's developed other problems as a result of a bad mouth.

Here is what to expect if you take your cat to have her teeth cleaned and her mouth assessed:

Dental diseases of all sorts are common in cats, especially as they age. Make sure your feline gets annual dental checkups.

- ❖ To begin, the veterinarian will perform a thorough physical examination, as well as check the general state of your cat's mouth to determine if there are any signs of tumors, bleeding, chipped teeth, gum disease, or periodontal disease.

- ❖ Dental X-rays will then be taken to help establish the degree of periodontal disease and the extent of bone destruction.

- ❖ Many veterinarians also recommend doing a blood panel. This will determine if any other problems exist internally that may affect kidney and liver functions before going ahead with the anesthesia needed to perform the actual cleaning. Anesthesia is necessary to ensure that your pet doesn't wriggle around while the veterinary technician performs the prophylaxis. (This is the official name of the treatment whereby the teeth are ultrasonically scaled to remove the plaque and then polished afterward.) This treatment is similar to what the dental hygienist performs in your mouth.

Because ATP stands for assessment, treatment, and prevention, when you come to fetch your fur kid, your veterinarian will the take time to discuss her mouth with you and give you advice on how to prevent any problems from reoccurring.

BEWARE OF "GENTLE DENTAL" TECHNIQUES

Only consider having your cat's teeth cleaned by a licensed veterinarian or dental technician at a veterinary office. Beware of unscrupulous people who offer anesthesia-free dental cleaning. Unlike Florida and California, many states do not have laws in place making this practice illegal.

More importantly, it's not possible for a cat to remain still without anesthesia. The instruments used are extremely sharp, and one slip can damage the gum line. Besides, a nonanesthetic teeth cleaning treatment can be a very stressful experience for a feline.

If possible, begin a dental care routine when your cat is young so she becomes accustomed to the process.

ROOT CANAL TREATMENTS

A root canal treatment is the recommended therapy for a fractured tooth. This is the procedure that removes the nerve substance completely. Unlike in dogs, crowns are not fitted to a cat's teeth to complete the procedure. Instead, veterinary dentists use special dental cement called gutta-percha, made from coagulated latex harvested from tropical rubber trees, to fill the gap left by the extracted tooth. The area is then permanently sealed with a special dental bonding material.

Feline tooth fractures frequently go unnoticed because they are not easy to detect. They are caused by trauma from being in a fight, being hit by car, or being kicked and abused. Often, adopted cats have fractured teeth, a badge of survival marking a tough life on the streets. My dearly beloved Muffin, who was the inspiration for this book, had a cracked lower incisor when I found her wandering around in a Cape mountain village in South Africa in 1994. My vet at the time told me there was nothing he could do about it. Thank goodness feline dentistry has come a long way since then.

We moved to California with our three cats in 1999, and Muffin lived out the rest of her life tended by the best veterinary care, which included regular dental checkups. However, she was plagued with dental problems, and looking back, I am sure that they originated with the initial care she received when she was first adopted. To this day, I feel guilty that she may have suffered as a result of my lack of general feline dental knowledge back then.

American pets are very lucky—they undoubtedly have the best care in the world available to them. As a responsible pet parent, it's up to you to see that your fur kid gets it.

COSMETIC DENTISTRY: ORTHODONTIC BRACES FOR FELINES

In dental terms, cats have what is called a scissor bite; when the mouth is closed, the upper incisors are in front of the lower incisors. Felines have different-shaped heads, and those with short muzzles, such as Persians, can suffer from maxillary canine teeth (the two top teeth that look like fangs) that project outward. This can cause eating problems. Also, if the teeth in any way damage the lip, infection that could in turn lead to periodontal disease may set in.

Under these circumstances, orthodontic braces can be used to correct bad bites. This is a specialized field, and your veterinarian will refer you to a veterinary orthodontist to rectify the matter.

Remember, you aren't doing this for vanity because you don't like Fluffy's smile; you're doing it to improve her quality of life. This type of procedure is rarely implemented in felines, but it's good to know that it can be performed if necessary. However, should your fur kid require braces, there's no color choice for orthodontic bands—they will be gray, like it or not!

DENTAL INSURANCE

Pet dental insurance is available through various animal medical insurance plans. However, I have often found that there are so many "ifs" and "buts" written into the average policy (the same with humans) that you may not be getting the best deal at the end of the day.

If you are unable to find a plan that suits your particular circumstances, initiate a special savings account for your feline at a bank of your choice rather than compromise your pet's dental and general health care by not being prepared. Shop around and find a bank that offers free checking. This way, it's not costing you anything to have the account. Also, an automatic monthly transfer from another banking account directly into this account eliminates the hassle of personally managing the money on a regular basis.

Do the math. For example, instead of paying premiums, deposit $50 per month into your pet savings account. The amount (with interest) will grow in excess of $6,000 over the next ten years, which should cover any dental (and medical problems) that may arise.

Dental checkups can be expensive, but you have to think long term. By doing regular teeth inspections and cleaning, you could be saving thousands of dollars down the road treating conditions that may have developed as a result of neglecting your cat's mouth. So effectively, the cost of teeth cleaning is priceless.

Bad Breath

A healthy cat's breath should not be offensive. And while not all cases of bad breath indicate a health problem, persistent halitosis can be a sign of tooth decay, which can lead to other dental and health issues:

- Bad breath similar to that of human halitosis may indicate periodontal disease.
- A sweet, fruity scent may indicate diabetes.
- A urine- or ammonia-like smell may indicate kidney disease.
- Foul odor associated with vomiting may indicate a liver disorder.

To prevent most cases of bad breath, clean your cat's teeth regularly and make sure that she gets a dental exam when she visits the vet for her annual checkup. Also, some veterinarians believe that dry food is better than canned food to prevent plaque buildup.

Chapter Six

Cat Nips and Tucks

Nose jobs, tummy tucks, breast reductions, eye lifts, ear shaping, and testicular implants. The list reads like the lineup for an extreme makeover television show but is in fact a record of cosmetic surgery procedures that can be performed on cats.

*T*echnically, these procedures are similar to those performed on people. But don't for one moment think that cosmetic surgery is a question of enhancing a floppy ear, improving a crooked smile, or absurdly trying to give a Persian cat a nose like Paris Hilton's.

It's not about appeasing feline parental vanity; we've already established that *all cats* are beautiful just they way they are. When talking about cosmetic surgery for pets, the focus should be on rectifying a genuine medical problem and eradicating any pain and suffering they may be enduring. Thus, in feline terms, plastic surgery is about improving your pet's well-being. As pet parents, we only want the best for our fur kids, and if you can afford it, it's a problem solver.

Cosmetic surgery procedures for pets focus on rectifying a genuine medical problem and eradicating any pain and suffering they may be enduring.

TUMMY TUCKS AND BOOB JOBS

Many cats who have not been spayed at the appropriate age or those who have been allowed to have too many litters are left with pendulous breast tissue. This is often the case with cats adopted from shelters. And like with post-pregnant women, the breasts do not naturally decrease in size.

In extreme cases, when breasts and tummies are literally dragging on the ground, impeding walking, playing, and life in general, surgery is the only way to alleviate the problem. This amounts to a tummy tuck and breast reduction to reduce tummy and breast tissue. In extreme cases, a mastectomy may also be necessary.

The risks are the same as they would be for any surgical procedure requiring anesthesia over a period of several hours. Your veterinarian will help you decide if this type of surgery is a proper and safe solution to your cat's particular problem.

COSMETIC FACIAL RESHAPING

Felines are known to have a high incidence of squamous cell carcinomas in the facial area such as the nose, lips, and ears. This type of cancer can eat away the nose, often warranting surgical removal of the nostrils, which will be done as cosmetically correct as possible. Veterinary surgeons do not make prosthetic snap-on noses to help things look more normal, though. It's not practical because the five-year remission period from cancer in people is equivalent to eight months in a cat. And in that timeframe, the cancer could have spread elsewhere. A skilled surgeon can also cosmetically trim a cancerous lip or symmetrically redefine ears to eradicate cancer.

As I have already mentioned, early detection can possibly prevent any of these drastic surgical procedures. The moment you notice anything unusual on the facial area, particularly on pink noses and ears, seek veterinary advice.

COSMETIC EAR PROCEDURES

An ear that's been damaged as a result of trauma or a cat fight can be cosmetically corrected, too. Surgeons can reconstruct the ear using cartilage from an area in the ear canal where it's never going to be noticed or missed. It "grows" in its new position, remodeling the ear to its former shape.

An alternative method involves implanting a special FDA-approved micro-thin silicone sheet specifically manufactured for pet implants. These ultra-thin sheets are reinforced with mesh webbing and can easily be surgically cut to any shape.

Many veterinarians are against the insertion of any synthetic materials. The final decision rests with you. But at least if you are aware of the options, you can knowledgeably discuss them with your veterinarian.

Liposuction

Feline obesity may be on the rise, but liposuction is *not* an option! The risks and potential side effects of the procedure are well documented. Treat the problem in the kitchen and not in the consulting room.

Proper age-related nutrition is the key to overall health maintenance and weight control. By selecting a diet specially designed to meet the nutritional needs of your cat based on her stage of life, you can improve her overall health and well-being and even add years to her life.

If your feline is excessively flabby, let your veterinarian supervise a serious weight-loss program. The food products sold by veterinarians are more specific in their ingredients so that your cat's nutritional needs will remain balanced as she loses weight.

A nose job can enlarge nostrils to make breathing easier.

NOSE JOBS

Certain cat breeds like Persians, Himalayans, and Angoras, which have "squished faces" and flat noses, are prone to breathing problems. A nose job can enlarge the nostrils in an attempt to make breathing easier. The procedure is called an alar fold resection and amounts to cutting back on the tissues and making the nostrils a little larger.

However, cats with this anatomical feature are often respiratorily challenged on a number of different levels. The nose itself is just the tip of the iceberg. In many cases, the cat may have an elongated soft palate at the back of the throat that makes the air passages narrower, or she may have a smaller trachea. X-rays, an endoscopic evaluation of the airways, and even a CT scan will allow your veterinary surgeon to make a proper evaluation.

EYE LIFTS

In the chapter on eye care (Chapter 4), I mentioned the problem of corneal damage being caused by the feline herpes virus and that in some cases, it's necessary to do surgery to ensure that the eyelashes do not rub against the cornea, causing further discomfort, damage, and even total blindness.

Entropian eye surgery, the procedure that prevents the eyelids from rolling inward and stops the eyelashes from rubbing the eye, is the equivalent of a cosmetic eye lift operation in humans. By lifting the brow and removing the skin folds that allow the eyebrows to droop, the problem is completely eradicated. Veterinarians say that pain associated with the operation wears off within a couple days.

SILICONE EYE IMPLANTS

In the past, veterinary surgeons simply sutured an eyelid closed if a pet lost an eye. Doing so resulted in a lopsided and rather unattractive face. Today, pet parents have another option: an FDA-approved silicone eye implant that has been made available for use with animals. This corrective procedure will definitely improve your cat's cosmetic appearance. Although it is not a replacement "eye," the implant allows the sutured eyelid to give the face a more balanced and less disfigured appearance.

As with all such procedures, this kind of decision needs to be made in conjunction with your vet and a veterinary ophthalmic surgeon.

TAIL IMPLANTS

A phenomenal number of tails gets caught in doors, drawers, and sadly, under car tires. Ouch! Further damage is done when the animal tries to pull free. In the old days, veterinary surgeons used to put the fractured tail in a splint or a cast. At worst, they would amputate it at the break. This often left a big, uncomfortable knot. Fortunately, surgeons can now make tails as good as new by implanting a thin titanium plate, the same as that used for human fingers, and then reconstructing the tail.

This type of reconstructive surgery will save the tail and free your fur kid from pain and discomfort. And of course, when the hair grows back, there will be no sign of the operation.

COSMETIC SKIN GRAFTS

As discussed, a scratch on the body that appears harmless may be an indication of skin cancer. Once again, it has usually spread considerably by the time it's brought to the attention of a veterinarian and is more than likely a situation requiring immediate surgical intervention. Veterinary reconstructive surgeons can perform cosmetic skin grafts on afflicted areas of the body to remove the cancerous skin and replace it with healthy skin.

Cosmetic skin grafts are also fairly common following some kind of trauma resulting from a car accident, a severe animal attack, or a burn from a car muffler. By doing muscular skeletal flaps or muscular cutaneous flaps, the surgeon takes the skin and the underlying subcutaneous

Foot Restoration

Recently, orthopedic and reconstructive surgeons at North Carolina State University College of Veterinary Medicine in Raleigh, North Carolina, performed groundbreaking surgery on a cat born without back feet. Using an osseointegrated implant, this technique involves inserting a thin steel shank into the leg bone that allows bone to grow around it in the same way it does around a hip replacement socket. The steel pin is then concealed by a cosmetic prosthetic closely resembling a cat's paw. If proven consistently successful, this surgery raises new hope for both animal and human amputees.

tissue and muscle and mobilizes it to cover the gaping skin wounds. Afterward, the fur grows back in its natural hair pattern, covering any signs of damage.

SCAR PREVENTION

Animals, like people, are prone to keloid and unsightly scarring, which can be uncomfortable and tender to the touch. And some doctors don't pay much attention when sewing their patients up either, leaving nasty scarring. At least cats are lucky because their fur can hide a multitude of sins!

Don't be shy to ask about suturing techniques that will prevent scar formation. Some years back, when I needed a major surgical procedure, the surgeon performing the operation was flabbergasted when I insisted on having a plastic surgeon stand by to complete the surgery. He later admitted that the cosmetic surgeon had paid far more attention to the internal stitching (as well as the visible suturing) than he normally would have. Small, delicate stitches also make it less painful and easier

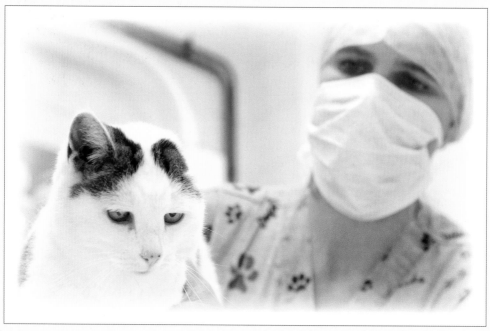

Reconstructive or corrective surgery can greatly enhance the quality of your fur kid's life, especially in cases of disfigurement caused by illness, accidents, or genetic abnormalities.

for the patient to move around soon afterward. This very same surgeon subsequently teamed up with a cosmetic surgeon on a permanent basis.

I would like to believe that a veterinary surgeon who takes the time and trouble to perform reconstructive procedures on your pet would consider the correct suture materials and suture patterns to minimize scarring. It doesn't cost anything to ask!

TESTICULAR IMPLANTS

For anthropomorphic cat owners who refuse to neuter their fur kid for fear of interfering with his masculinity, there are cosmetic feline testicular implants available. You can even have special implants made that replicate your cat's own testicles, although at a price!

These vanity implants can be inserted during the neutering operation. There are many different sizes and textures available. They have a special casing that prevents scar tissue from developing around them.

Before You Decide

Cosmetic surgery procedures for pets are not purely elective procedures, as they may be for humans. There has to be a very good medical reason to put your animal companion under the knife. Besides, a dedicated veterinary reconstructive surgeon will never consider doing a procedure just to appease feline parental vanity.

Only consider a procedure if it's going to rectify a genuine medical problem, eradicate pain, and improve your fur kid's quality of life. Discuss the pros and cons of performing the surgery with your veterinarian before making a final decision.

In all honesty, fur kids who don't have a career in the show ring and who aren't part of a breeding program should be neutered. It's the responsible thing to do. By leaving your tom's testosterone-charged manhood alone, you stand the chance of knowingly or inadvertently adding to the unwanted pet population.

THE PRICE YOU PAY FOR RECONSTRUCTIVE SURGERY

Depending on the situation and immediate needs of your pet, cost can often be a major concern because reconstructive procedures are expensive. Typical ear surgery, a rhinoplasty, or an abdominoplasty call for the experience and expertise of a board-certified veterinary surgeon. More than likely, your fur kid will also require overnight hospitalization so that she can be properly monitored after anesthesia.

If you feel that such surgery, although warranted, may be financially prohibitive, do not be embarrassed to discuss your situation with the vet's office. Most are willing to structure a personal payment plan that will keep you from delaying necessary surgery.

Obviously, testicular implants don't fall in this category. Such is the price of pure vanity!

Chapter Seven

The Spaw Experience

The mere sight of the carrier coming out of the closet is usually enough to send most cats running to hide under the bed—just a couple millimeters out of reach, of course! In the feline world, the carrier is usually equated with two things: a visit to the vet or a trip to the grooming salon, or "pet spaw."

A visit to the groomer is understandably traumatic because most establishments take block bookings, which means that on arrival, kitty is placed in a cage to wait her turn and then has to endure endless barking from yappy doggy clients. And all this before the nail clippers are even removed from the sterilizer and the actual grooming session officially begins!

CHOOSING A GROOMER YOUR FUR KID LIKES

Imagine a visit to your hairdresser if there was no casual chat to lather things up or gossip to spritz up the occasion. In a nutshell, the perfect human stylist is someone who can offer and execute good advice while at the same time be easy to talk to. All these things make the appointment a relaxing and enjoyable experience.

Well, pets appreciate the same comforts you do. If you decide to leave your fur kid's grooming to a professional, you'll want a groomer who will listen to your requests, make recommendations that will improve the health and well-being of your pet, and most importantly, talk to and comfort your pet. This may sound silly, but remember, your cat isn't sitting and reading the latest magazines and drinking lattes to relax, so a friendly voice will make all the difference in an unfamiliar and stressful environment.

Pets appreciate the same comforts people do, so choose a groomer who will talk to and comfort your cat during the grooming session.

Before choosing a facility, don't be shy about asking to see the grooming area. Inquire what kind of products and dryers are used, and speak up! For instance, if your pet cringes at the sight of a handheld hair dryer, a cage dryer may be the answer. Some groomers do work by appointment, so your cat won't have to be caged for hours beforehand. Ask for information about the full range of services offered. And if you don't "bond," go elsewhere. As with human stylists, personal recommendations are often the best.

CAT-ONLY GROOMERS

The best way to find a groomer who specializes in cats is to ask your veterinarian or inquire at your local pet boutique. Cat shows are another great source of local information.

As far as I am concerned, the perfect feline groomer is someone who is a cat person first and a groomer second. Such a person will understand your feline and make the whole experience as enjoyable as possible while getting the beauty routine done quickly and efficiently. Also, try to find a "cats-only" groomer. He will have lots of experience dealing with cats, and your feline won't be frightened or distracted by the scents and sounds of dogs or other animals in the establishment.

As the industry changes, many grooming salons are taking on a much more "human feel" and consider themselves pet beauty parlors or "pet spaws." They pamper their four-legged clients accordingly with "peticures," ear and teeth cleaning, touchup work on facial stains, and even full-body massages. Find out what a day at a spa near you entails; it may be worth it to indulge your favorite feline. Websites such as www.findagroomer.com list establishments countrywide. Many pet stores, such as Petco and PetSmart, and pet hotels offer grooming services, too. However, some don't groom cats at all or won't groom cats over the age of ten because they don't react well in a noisy grooming environment. However, in

Haircuts: Turning Your Pussycat Into a Lion

If your cat is going to a professional groomer, you may be wondering: What about special haircuts for felines? Unlike dogs, styling your cat doesn't involve a choice of various haircuts. However, there are occasions when you may want to consider shaving your longhaired beauty completely or giving her a lion cut by leaving a ruff of fur around her neck and possibly a little fluffy brush at the tip of her tail. For example, a lion cut works well in hot climates to keep cats cool and mat-free and should always be done by a professional groomer with the right tools. Never wait until your kitty's coat is extremely tangled and matted before you decide on the lion cut. This will only make the grooming experience more of an ordeal. Keeping fur short is also an excellent option for elderly longhaired kitties who are no longer adept in attending to their own beauty routines.

Cropped fur can benefit pet parents, too. While there are many wonderful products that control dander and significantly reduce human allergic reactions, giving your longhaired beauty a lion cut may also significantly help limit allergies if someone in your household is constantly sneezing.

consideration of fussy felines, others will allow you to stay with your cat throughout the service for an additional charge. So be sure to ask!

MOBILE GROOMING SPAS

If you truly want to pamper your cat with a "spaw" experience but she's too skittish leaving home, consider booking an appointment with a groomer who makes house calls—also known as a mobile grooming spa. Grooming packages may cost a little more, but at least you won't have to spend money on gas driving to and from the facility, let alone factor in the value of the time spent doing so. The biggest bonus is that you will spare your fur kid the stress and indignity of having to witness what is often some pretty unruly canine behavior while she waits her turn. Of course, there's no avoiding your fur kid's stress over being put into a carrier because it's the safest way to transport her from the security of your home to the mobile grooming station, but at least it will be a short trip.

Generally, mobile groomers will allow you to accompany your nervous kitty until she is settled in and then will ask you to come back when services are finished. They also often play soft, meditative music and spray lavender in the air before your cat's arrival to create an overall atmosphere of peace and calm. Because experienced groomers are sensitive to their nervous clients, they will start the session by slowly talking to and stroking your cat to invite her to come out of the carrier onto the table. They know that any groomer who turns the carrier upside down to pour a reluctant cat onto the worktable will never build a relationship with a feline client. And if kitty is a bit hesitant, a caring groomer will undo the top section of the carrier and gently remove her.

If you'd like to explore this option, you can learn more about the services offered by an upscale mobile groomer by researching online. Just Four Paws (www.justfourpaws.net) and Amber's Mobile Pet Salons (www.ambersmobilepetsalons.com) are two such providers, the latter being nationwide.

THE PROFESSIONAL SPA EXPERIENCE

Professional cat groomers, whether they work in standard or mobile salons, usually offer the same kinds of services. Again, if you are going to a regular salon, select one that works on an appointment-only basis. This means that your fur kid can avoid having to sit in a holding cage for hours waiting her turn, which can be very stressful for her.

Caution: Bump Up Ahead!

If your feline has any lumps or bumps on her body, identify them for the groomer with colored stickers. In the meantime, during your regular grooming sessions at home, prevent mishaps by simply putting your thumb on the lump or bump and carefully working around this tender spot.

THE GROOMING SESSION

Most grooming sessions start with

Besides offering top-notch services, a professional groomer will often make recommendations that will improve the health and well-being of your pet.

a pedicure to trim all the nails and the dewclaws, followed by an ear cleaning with cotton swabs dipped in an antiseptic cleaner. Next, your cat will receive a teeth cleaning using a dental cleaning tip or the kind that fits on a finger.

When nail, ear, and dental care have been completed, it's time for a thorough brushing. The groomer will brush the fur and detangle any mats using a deshedding tool that has both long and short teeth to remove loose hair from the topcoat as well as the undercoat.

If brushing makes kitty nervous, some groomers will use a harness that resembles a mail carrier's bag—it fits across the cat's chest and under one armpit. In severe cases, it may even be necessary to use a feline muzzle, which also covers the eyes. Cats usually calm down when they can't see what's happening. It's the same concept as putting a cover over a bird cage.

Once the coat is brushed and detangled, it's bath time. An experienced groomer will put the water on ahead of time to allow your cat to get accustomed to the sound of it running. Before putting her in the bath, he will spray a bit of water on her to see how she reacts. This is important because once shampoo is applied, the groomer needs to know that he will have sufficient time to

If you have plans to show your cat, you must learn to groom her yourself.

rinse it off properly; soapy residue left behind could cause itching and skin problems. A very wriggly cat will probably prefer being bathed with a waterless shampoo mousse, which is removed with warm, wet towels.

Either way, the bath session will be from the neck down. The face will be excluded, and the groomer will simply wipe it with a warm cloth so that kitty never gets water in her eyes.

For those felines who will tolerate a bath, no doubt the best part is being wrapped in a warm comfy towel afterward and being taken back to the grooming table to be dried off. A lot of groomers prefer using a leave-in conditioner, which they massage into the skin and fur and comb through.

ADDITIONAL BODY SERVICES

These days, many professional pet groomers are trained in various health and well-being modalities such as massage or Reiki, and it is at this point in the spaw session that they will set to work for about 20 minutes of hands-on, soothing touch therapy. What cat doesn't enjoy a gentle rubdown? The types of additional massage services that can be offered and their benefits are detailed in Chapter 9.

SIGNING OUT

Before being placed back in the carrier to return home, final touches may include a spritz of lavender spray and perhaps a pretty bow attached to kitty's collar. The groomer may even give her a toy such as a ball or a catnip mouse to ensure that the grooming session has been a positive experience.

It's not necessary to make monthly appointments for your fur kid. Because cats are excellent self-cleaning machines, a visit to the groomer is probably only necessary every 8 to 12 weeks.

GROOMING FOR SHOW CATS

If you have plans to show your cat, you must learn to groom her yourself because the average salon doesn't have the time or the knowledge relating to the standard requirements for individual breeds. It can take up to three hours to prepare a cat for the show ring!

People in the cat show world are very helpful in this regard. Start by speaking with the breeder who sold you your kitten. You can also find out what judges are looking for in the show ring by reading the breed standard, which you can find on the Cat Fanciers' Association (CFA) website www.cfa.org or on the websites of other similar organizations.

Taking Senior Felines to the Spa

Some pet parents may find it challenging to safely and properly groom an older pet. Great patience and skill are necessary to ensure that she remains comfortable and secure while being handled. For this reason, many owners may prefer to pay a professional pet groomer to tend to their aging cat's grooming needs.

Choose a groomer who is friendly and patient and who takes the time to ensure that your cat has a good experience. Make sure that he has expertise dealing with older animals. Ask to tour the facility (it must be clean), and see if the groomer will let you watch him groom someone else's cat to see how he interacts with and handles an older animal. Get references from all the groomers you visit, and check them.

When you find a groomer you'd like to use, ask if he will allow you to stay and watch how the process is done. If you like what you see, make an appointment for a first-time visit. Talk to your senior in a soothing voice if she becomes scared or nervous. If your cat becomes very upset, you may have to consider trying to groom her at home yourself, or perhaps your vet can refer you to a reliable at-home grooming service.

Chapter Eight

Aromatherapy and Flower Essences for Feline Well-Being

These days, the focus of our lifestyle is about exploring a more natural and holistic approach to attaining general good health. And in our quest to enjoy the love and companionship of our fur kids for as long as possible, it follows that we want them to experience the same therapeutic benefits derived from the slew of treatments and remedies that instill both a zest for living and a sense of calm. Indubitably, aromatherapy tops the list.

WHAT IS AROMATHERAPY?

When I started writing this chapter, I did an impromptu survey to find out what people perceived aromatherapy to be all about. The answers included everything from natural-ingredient shampoos and nice-smelling candles to a really good body massage.

Well, it's all those things and more! To be specific, aromatherapy is a generic term that refers to the various uses of liquid plant materials known as essential oils for the purpose of affecting a person or animal's mood or health. These oils are extracted from flowers and other plant compounds such as leaves, stems, roots, seeds, and bark. And apart from being mood enhancers, they have various medicinal and healing properties and thus promote general well-being. Essential oils have actually been around for centuries and are still widely used by many cultures as part of their medicinal and spiritual beliefs.

Next time you have friends over and everyone's relaxing over a glass of wine and enjoying the fragrance of the aromatherapy candles you're burning (and your fur kid snoozes happily in your favorite chair!), here's a bit of conversational trivia that's bound to impress.

The word "aromatherapy" was coined as recently as the 1920s by a French chemist named René-Maurice Gattefossé. The story, now quoted as historical fact, relates how he was working on formulations in his perfume laboratory when he accidentally set fire to his arm. He grabbed the nearest cold liquid to pour on his skin, which happened to be a vat of lavender oil, and was amazed that it instantly relieved the intense pain. Further, he noticed that the burn healed remarkably quickly without the usual redness, blistering, and scarring he'd experienced from previous mishaps in his laboratory. After that, Gattefossé started researching the properties of other essential oils, which are now ubiquitous in our daily lives.

HOW AROMATHERAPY WORKS

Aromatherapists believe that essential oils work in two ways. First, the fragrant aromas activate the limbic system and stimulate the emotional centers of the brain. Second, when applied to the skin, they are absorbed into the bloodstream, thereby allowing the body to register them and promote healing.

This translates into the current trend for environmental fragrancing. A whole industry of topical uses has been developed for therapeutic skin care products, various other cosmetic preparations such as bathing additives, and of course, massage oils. Flower essences are even used in health-related products. For example, some anti-itch creams used to treat skin irritations contain chamomile oil, and some insect repellents use lavender oil as an ingredient.

WORDS OF WARNING

All this being said, when it comes to using aromatherapy on cats, this therapeutic euphoria is punctuated with words of extreme caution. Essential oils are very concentrated and hence extremely potent; a little goes a long way. They should never be administered full strength to either humans or animals because they can do more harm than good in this form.

Undiluted essential oils are highly toxic to cats. Even one drop on your cat's paw can make her extremely ill and may even cause death. Unlike humans and even dogs, felines lack the necessary enzymes in their liver to break down and excrete certain chemical compounds that exist naturally in essential oils. Therefore, overdosing or overuse causes these compounds to accumulate in the body and can result in liver or kidney failure.

Symptoms of toxicity include vomiting, drooling, and uncoordinated movements. The toxic buildup is often slow and doesn't necessarily show up immediately. It could take weeks, months, or even years. Often, owners are unaware that their cat is suffering from any kind of poisoning until the vet does a general blood panel and it shows up there.

Fortunately, you can buy ready-made dilutions of essential oils called hydrosols. These are water-based by-products that can be diluted even further for safe use. Before you proceed, consult a professional pet aromatherapist with regard to formulations for your cat and how to correctly administer them.

I apologize for lecturing. But it's important to spell this all out in the interest of feline safety.

Aromatherapy is used to treat common emotional or behavioral issues your cat may be facing due to stress, loneliness, grief, or separation anxiety.

HYDROSOLS

If René-Maurice Gattefossé is the father of modern-day aromatherapy, then Canadian aromatherapist Suzanne Catty is the mother of hydrosol aromatherapy. She is the author of *Hydrosols: The Next Aromatherapy* and has done extensive research into the subject of felines and hydrosols. She claims that true therapeutic hydrosols, free of preservatives, alcohol, and stabilizers, are a safe choice for cats.

THERAPEUTIC AND FEEL-GOOD BENEFITS FOR CATS

When it comes to felines, apart from getting rid of parasites such as ticks and fleas, aromatherapy is used to treat mild skin inflammations, sore muscles, and stiff joints. It's also used to de-stress a variety of emotionally charged situations, such as traveling, moving, the introduction of a new pet or baby into a household, separation anxiety, and nervousness induced by thunder and lightning storms. While the hydrosols can be used individually, pet aromatherapists often blend several together.

Consult a professional pet aromatherapist about which hydrosol formulations your cat can use and how to correctly administer them.

POPULAR ESSENTIAL OIL HYDROSOLS AND THEIR USES

The following are the most commonly used hydrosols for cats:

- **Cedarwood** is known to help calm emotions, especially in animals who have suffered trauma. Because it also dispels parasites such as fleas and ticks, it's used in kitty litter (cedar chips) as well as in bedding.
- **Cornflower** is excellent for treating dry, flaky skin conditions.
- **Eucalyptus** is good for respiratory ailments as well as for soothing sore muscles. It's also recognized for its antiseptic properties.
- **Geranium** is listed as an antidepressant and is used to help clear toxins and waste matter from the body. Its anti-inflammatory properties are great for all kinds of skin conditions.
- **Lavender** is widely recognized to work on both a physical level to relax muscles and on

an emotional level to relax, de-stress, and relieve anxiety. Because it has both cooling and healing properties, it's excellent for burns and skin irritations.

- **Lemon verbena** is known for its stress-relieving properties. It also has anti-inflammatory properties and is often used to treat teeth and gum infections.
- **Neroli**, commonly known as orange blossom, is used as a mild sedative on pets and thus is a popular choice to treat stress and emotional disorders.
- **Roman chamomile** is used to calm and relax an overexcited or nervous animal. It is excellent for separation anxiety and also has excellent skin healing properties.
- **Rose** is used for sensitive skin conditions such as rashes, as well as for bites, scratches, and cuts.
- **Rosemary** is a popular flea repellent. Because of its wonderful fresh scent, it's often used as a deodorizer.
- **Vetiver** is considered a natural tranquilizer and is used for relieving stress and helping animals recover from emotional trauma and shock.
- **Witch hazel** has anti-inflammatory properties similar to a topical steroid cream. It also has wonderful antioxidant properties, which can help heal topical cuts and scratches quickly.

[A word of warning: Never use pennyroyal oil on pets because it is highly toxic in any form.]

HOW TO INTRODUCE YOUR CAT TO HYDROSOLS

Let's do a one-minute quiz to test your general knowledge about your cat's nose.

Why do cats frequently appear to turn up their noses at food?

- (a) They're checking to see whether it's the same food you served the night before.
- (b) They have a very keen sense of smell.
- (c) It's just a twitch and means nothing.

The answer is (b).

A cat's nose is undoubtedly her most important organ. Cats have between 60 and 80 million olfactory cells, while humans have only between 5 and 20 million, which explains their incredible sense of smell. They also have a special scent organ called the Jacobson's organ, located in the palate. It analyzes every smell, and when it's working, cats often appear to be "tasting" the air—that's why it often looks as if they are turning up their noses to food!

Cats depend on their sense of smell for their very survival and instinctively know which smells are good for

Caution Necessary

In their pure form, essential oils contain naturally formed chemicals known as phenols and ketones, which are harmful to cats. The list of oils that contain these chemicals includes oregano, thyme, clove, cinnamon, savory birch, melaleuca (tea tree oil), and sage, as well as citrus oils, pine, spruce, and any fir oils. However, phenols and ketones are not present in the hydrosol formulations of these oils.

them and which ones to avoid. And this is particularly true when it comes to introducing them to essential oil hydrosols. Consequently, pet aromatherapists suggest that the best way to introduce your cat to a particular oil is to allow her to first sniff it and watch for signs of acceptance. If your fur kid instantly gets up and stalks off, that's a clue not to proceed. If she shows interest by wanting to lick or by rubbing against it, you can take this as a sign that the hydrosol in question will have a therapeutic effect and that your cat is giving you the green light to proceed. Never test a hydrosol by placing it on your cat's nose because this takes away her freedom of choice.

Before you brush off this advice as just another fishy cat tale, this principal is endorsed by Caroline Ingraham of the Ingraham Animal Aromatic Science and Research Centre in the United Kingdom. For more than two decades, Ingraham has studied aromatherapy essential oils as well as other plant extracts and their symbiotic relationship to animals. She is a world authority and supports the principle that animals have the innate ability to select remedies similar to those that they would seek in the wild and that they guide the dosage they require to be healed. She cites big wild cats in their natural habitat rolling on selected plants and inhaling the fragrance released by this action.

Pet aromatherapists suggest that the best way to introduce your cat to a particular essential oil hydrosol is to allow her to first sniff it, then watch for signs of acceptance.

Further, Ingraham says that once an animal has selected her remedy, she will then guide the treatment, and when the condition has cleared or improved, will reject aromas that were previously chosen and enjoyed.

Simply put, listen to your cat!

HOW TO APPLY OR GIVE HYDROSOLS

You can apply hydrosols to the paw pads, the tips of the ears, or the shoulder blades. In the case of stiff joints, they should be applied directly to the area and massaged in gently. Instead of massage, you can place a warm towel over the area and allow the oils to be absorbed into the bloodstream. You can also place a few drops of the diluted hydrosol in a saucer and allow your pet to inhale the properties; this is called cold-diffusion. Make sure, of course, that your cat does not ingest the solution, and remove the saucer when treatment is finished. Another method is to spritz the hydrosol on pet bedding and other areas where your pet likes to snooze.

[A word of caution: Never place hydrosols directly in the eyes or in the ears.]

FINDING A PET AROMATHERAPIST

Before using any kind of in-home treatment on your cat, it's always best to first consult your vet, or in this case, a professional aromatherapist. The National Association for Holistic Aromatherapists (NAHA) is a good place to seek out a qualified pet therapist because members are required to have specific certification to be accepted by the organization. You can find out more about them on their website at www.naha.org.

If you're considering an initial consultation and thereafter plan to continue treatments at home, consider asking the therapist to professionally blend the correct hydrosol solutions for your home use. However, should you be given the names of the hydrosol formulations and intend to buy them yourself, shop at holistic pet stores or on websites that specialize in hydrosols for pets. Because there is no regulating body overseeing the manufacture and distribution of these products, you must read the labels carefully to ensure that you are in fact buying hydrosols that are made from genuine and not synthetic formulations.

Both the actual essential oils and their hydrosol formulations are expensive because particular oils are only grown in certain parts of the world, and putting them in a bottle is a costly process. Look for words like "therapeutic grade" or "steam distillate waters" on the bottle, or indications of the country of origin.

Hydrosols are best kept in a cool place out of direct sunlight, even refrigerated. Generally speaking, their efficacy lasts six months.

FLOWER ESSENCES: A DIFFERENT BALL OF STRING

People very often get confused between essential oils and flower essences—probably because "essential" and "essence" are both "e" words. But they are totally different modalities, and flower essences are quite safe to use on cats.

First, flower essences (also known as flower remedies) are fragrance-free. By definition, they are high-frequency electrical solutions distilled from fresh flower blossoms. These essences contain the distinct vibrational energies of the plants from which they are derived, and when properly applied, they help balance and strengthen the body's electrical system. In doing so, they remove any interference that can cause both physical and emotional discomfort. Simply put, they can alleviate both physical pain and discomfort and emotionally work to relieve stress.

The most famous of all flower essences are those formulated by British physician Dr. Edward Bach in the 1930s. He created 38 different essences, all of which are perfectly safe to use on cats—including his famous Rescue Remedy calmative, which is a combination of several of his key floral essences.

Naturally, other companies have tried to duplicate these remedies over the years, and various names are now available worldwide. But Dr. Bach's are undoubtedly world famous. Twenty-seven of the individual essences, including his famous Rescue Remedy, are particularly beneficial to pets:

- ❖ **Aspen** is used to treat vague accountable fears in cats, such as skittish behavior or appearing agitated for no apparent reason, by providing a sense of security in their environment.

- ❖ **Beech** is used to treat intolerance of other animals or people.

- ❖ **Cherry plum** helps quell violent scratching and induces calm self-control.

- ❖ **Chestnut bud** helps change unwanted behavioral patterns and allows the animal to make adjustments more comfortably.

- ❖ **Chicory** is used on manipulative and territorial cats to produce a more self-assured frame of mind.

Flower essences can alleviate physical pain and discomfort and emotionally work to relieve stress.

✤ **Clematis** helps shy animals who have no apparent interest in things around them to develop a more lively interest in the home environment and the other pets and people who share their space.

✤ **Crab apple** helps animals who obsessively groom to relax and not be overly fastidious.

✤ **Elm** helps mother cats who are overwhelmed with the responsibility of a litter from possibly abandoning her kittens, allowing her to relax and cope better.

✤ **Gentian** helps cats deal with despondency that may occur as a result of a change in a standard routine.

✤ **Heather** is useful for cats who are particularly clingy and who want companionship all the time.

✤ **Holly** helps cats overcome jealousy of other animals or a new baby and also helps quell constant hissing.

✤ **Honeysuckle** helps overcome homesickness if the cat has been taken out of her home environment and needs to adjust to a new setting.

✤ **Hornbeam** restores lethargy and a lack of enthusiasm.

✤ **Impatiens** helps control boundless energy and frantic rushing around the house, allowing the feline to become more patient and relaxed.

✤ **Larch** helps boost a cat's self-esteem and confidence, especially in households where there are other pets.

✤ **Mimulus** works to quell fear of storms and visits to the vet. It also generally helps shy and timid cats become more relaxed and confident.

✤ **Olive** helps show animals who may be suffering from exhaustion and fatigue by restoring strength and vitality.

✤ **Rescue Remedy** is a combination of chestnut, Star of Bethlehem, clematis, cherry plum,

Stress-Free Travel

If you have a fussy feline who hates riding in the car—and most do—flower essences can make traveling less stressful for her, especially if the trip is more than a couple hours long. And it couldn't be simpler! All you do is add Rescue Remedy to your cat's water bowl and freeze it. This way, it will slowly melt en route and she will be able to have the ongoing benefits of the remedy throughout the journey.

Many veterinarians believe that this is a much better alternative than actually tranquilizing your pet because if the effects of the tranquilizer wear off during the journey, the animal may become even more stressed and emotionally overwrought by the situation.

impatiens, and rock rose. It is used to combat any stressful situation, such as visits to the vet, a fear of being left alone, adapting to new surroundings, and loud noises. It works to calm a cat who is excessively stressed and hissing as well. Rescue Remedy is also great for calming pets during travel and is used to deal with trauma and shock from an accident or natural disaster.

- ❖ **Rock rose** helps reduce signs of terror and panic that can prompt an animal to hide or run away from people.
- ❖ **Scleranthus** is used to treat cats who cannot make up their minds to become more decisive.
- ❖ **Star of Bethlehem** helps cats who have been abused or mistreated in the past to better deal with their present situation.
- ❖ **Vervain** helps highly strung cats calm down and relax.
- ❖ **Vine** encourages cats who try to dominate their owners to be more submissive.
- ❖ **Walnut** helps an animal adjust to a new environment and accept changes in the home.
- ❖ **Water violet** essence is used on unfriendly, standoffish cats who do not enjoy being petted and cuddled, coaxing them to become more sociable.
- ❖ **Wild oat** works well on cats who are no longer involved in show competitions and who feel as though they have lost their sense of purpose—it helps them adjust to being house cats.
- ❖ **Wild rose** restores natural energy and enthusiasm.

HOW TO TREAT YOUR CAT WITH FLOWER ESSENCES

Because all flower essences are completely safe, you can put a few drops directly into your cat's mouth using a dropper or add them to the water bowl. Because of the safety of flower essences, you cannot harm your cat by overdosing or by administering the wrong remedy.

As discussed, the benefits of these therapies are multifaceted, but they can be used for simple daily concerns or just to keep your pet healthy and happy. They are nontoxic, easy to use, and have no side effects—and they'll make life better for your fur kid and you.

Although you may find numerous websites devoted to alternative therapies for felines, it's always best to discuss use of any remedies or treatments with your vet before trying them on your cat. In the case of flower essences, which are generally safe, your cat will let you know which ones *she* prefers you use. In the case of essential oils, however, a professional aromatherapist or holistic vet is your best source of information. He can discuss the different remedies and treatments with you in detail so that you can be certain to offer your fur kid the best results possible.

"A" Is for Aromatherapy

If you are keen to learn more about aromatherapy for your fur kid, there are plenty of workshops held around the country. But if you don't have time to take a class, the following organizations can offer reliable and helpful information:

The National Association for Holistic Aromatherapists (NAHA)
3327 W. Indian Trail Road PMB 144
Spokane, WA 99208
Telephone: 509-325-3419
Website: www.naha.org

American Holistic Veterinary Medical Association (AHVMA)
2214 Old Emmorton Road
Bel Air, MD 21015
Telephone: 410-569-0795
Website: www.ahvma.org

The Dr. Edward Bach Foundation
Mount Vernon
Bakers Lane
Sotwell
Oxon, OX10 0PZ
United Kingdom
Telephone: +44-1491-834678
Website: www.bachcentre.com

If you are unsure which flower essences would be best for your cat under particular circumstances, Bach Flower remedies offers an online consultation service, which you can contact at consultation@bachflower.com. This service requires a fee, which can be paid by credit card.

Consider an aromatherapy session at home as a wonderful way to spend quality time with your pet. And it goes without saying that you will automatically benefit from the hydrosols you are working with, too.

Chapter Nine

MMMeow... Massage

MMM...good. That's what massage is all about. It's that universal feel-good sensation evoked by the simple power of touch. And in the animal kingdom, no animal understands the power of physical communication better than the domestic cat. After all, nothing puts a feline into purr mode quicker than lightly laying your hands on her body, stroking her under the chin, tickling her ears or her tummy, or even gently pulling her tail.

*A*s a besotted pet parent, you probably massage your cat every day without stopping to think about your actions. Yes—petting is massage and massage is petting. So is there a difference? Yes, there is. According to W. Bruce Bregenzer, one of America's leading proponents of animal massage, the main difference between the two is the masseur's or masseuse's intent.

For your stroking and petting movements to be officially considered a pet massage, the intent has to be to touch the animal for some beneficial effect. Further, Bregenzer points out that for this to occur, the cat has to give you permission to perform a therapeutic touching routine. And most cats don't beat about the bush on this one! If they're interested in pursuing the idea, they will automatically nuzzle up to you, lie down, or simply stay where they are—all obvious indications that they're giving you, or a professional pet massage therapist, the go-ahead to continue. And just to let you know that you've mastered the art, they'll purr or sometimes even rumble in contentment. Some felines will close their eyes to savor the moment. Others will lick your hand, knead your lap, or even give you gentle love bites.

By the same token, all felines have the right to say no. The most obvious rejection is to jump up and run off, possibly heading under the bed or on top of a high bookshelf and making it very clear that you are not to follow! Your feline may even turn her back on you and begin a vigorous inspection of her nails, followed by an intense manicure. She may even grab your hand, and while

No animal understands the power of physical communication better than the domestic cat.

she has you in her grip, sink a fang or two into it. To summarize, you will definitely get the message on massage.

Pet massage therapists explain that felines offer such clear-cut reactions to the prospect of a massage because they are really in tune with their bodies and know how they are supposed to feel. Consequently, they instinctively know when something is wrong. If something is out of alignment, they tend to compensate in their movements, and because they are such stoic creatures, will hide their pain well. It's easy for a massage therapist to explain to a human patient how a massage can improve their well-being. But with a cat, you are basically relying on their instinctual trust, which allows them to give you the opportunity to try to help. And if they are not quite ready for the change, they won't let you touch them. It's as simple as that.

That's why massage therapists always start off with gentle petting strokes, just as you would do on a daily basis out of pure love and affection. Once they see how the cat reacts to the idea, they know whether to proceed with a "routine of intent."

THERAPEUTIC BENEFITS FOR FELINES

It goes without saying that the power of touch is very soothing and encourages relaxation, which in turn relieves tension and stress. This translates into emotional, social, and behavioral benefits for felines.

Massage improves blood circulation, increasing oxygenation and nutrition to the cells and tissues throughout the body. If your fur kid is on any medication, massage will help it work more efficiently, and at the same time, minimize any side effects by removing the toxins and waste products from the system. Increased blood circulation also reduces pain associated with illness or old age because endorphins, the body's natural pain relievers, are released into the system. These natural mood enhancers allow your feline to feel better. In human terms, this translates into an upbeat mood. The gentle power of touch also releases lactic acid from sore muscles, decreasing swelling from inflammation. It definitely allows older cats suffering from arthritis and joint discomfort more flexibility of movement and could possibly help them negotiate stairs around the home well into their teens.

While massage therapy is no substitute for veterinary care, more veterinarians are appreciating the benefits and seeing how it complements medical treatments. Thus, they are recommending massage therapy for cats who have undergone surgery or some kind of trauma from abuse to help facilitate the healing process.

If your fur kid has a career in the feline show ring, a massage could greatly improve her feeling of well-being, reduce any emotional stress that she may be picking up from you, invigorate her muscles, and generally improve her performance in front of the judges, resulting in another ribbon to add to the trophy room.

Massage for Seniors

It's becoming more common for pet parents to treat elderly cats to a regular "maintenance massage." If you maintain flexibility and ensure that the blood flow is good and keeps toxins and waste matter out of the system, your cat will enjoy a healthier life and generally be more mobile as she ages. Often, a therapist will include other modalities during a treatment, such as some acupressure or healing touch therapy.

Professional pet massage therapists are capable of treating conditions such as arthritis. However, when it comes to medical issues, they prefer to take instructions from a veterinarian. I would strongly recommend this line of action.

And of course, there's one more very important aspect: The spin-off benefits for you! We've ascertained that there's no greater way to improve that bond between pet parent and fur kid than by gently stroking her. But in performing these gentle actions, you are in fact lowering your own blood pressure and stress levels, improving your personal health and well-being, too. Once again, it really is a win-win situation.

DIFFERENT STROKES

There are about 20 basic massage and touch techniques, including Swedish massage, shiatsu, Thai, hot stone therapy, reflexology, Reiki, Esalen massage, Tuina Chinese massage (acupressure), and many more. Every day there is something new because therapists blend, borrow, and vary patterns.

Pet massage therapists draw from all these modalities and put their own personal stamp on the massage technique they offer, taking cues from the animals themselves as to what they will tolerate and enjoy. However, the most common techniques employed by most pet massage therapists come from Swedish massage, which uses long, flowing strokes designed to increase circulation and blood flow and to limber up joins and relax tense muscles.

There are several basic strokes:

- ❖ **effleurage:** gliding strokes designed to warm up the muscles
- ❖ **petrissage:** gentle kneading and circular strokes
- ❖ **friction:** deep, circular rubbing
- ❖ **tapotement:** rhythmic tapping, administered in several ways—with the edge of the palm, the heel of the hand, the fingers, or with short, rapid movements using the sides of the hand
- ❖ **vibration movements:** very fine, rapid shaking

When used on people, Swedish massage is considered to be a deep-tissue massage. However, when it comes to working with cats, therapists adapt these stokes by applying a much lighter touch. Cats have several layers of muscles, as do humans; the pet massage therapist simply relaxes the first layer and gradually works deeper, without using any intense pressure, to reach the lower levels of muscle to achieve the same results.

A PROFESSIONAL PET MASSAGE SESSION

Many pet therapists prefer to come to their client's home. This has distinct advantages.

First, your fur kid will not be stressed by having to get into her carrier and journey to the appointment. Second, cats are definitely more relaxed and in tune with their own environment, which makes it easier for the therapist to work more efficiently.

PREPARATION

The initial appointment will kick off with the therapist asking you a lot of questions about your fur kid's general health. Provide as much specific information as you can about issues you'd like addressed during the session. If your veterinarian suggested such treatments, it's a good idea to ask the office to detail the problems to make it easier for the therapist to target those concerns.

Most therapists let the cat tell them in what area of the home they would like to be massaged, and a dedicated therapist will follow your fur kid around until she has located the spot of choice. And it can be anywhere—on your bed, on a kitchen countertop, or on your computer desk. She may even choose the therapist's lap if she is particularly social and enjoys this kind of interaction.

However, if it's a case of Goldilocks and the three bears, and your fur kid has tried out various places and deemed them too high, too soft, too low, and simply not right and stalks off, the session will end before it really began. Remember, this can happen at any time. For example, your cat may happily allow the therapist to work on three or four consecutive occasions and then suddenly decide that a massage isn't on the agenda for the day, dismissing the therapist with a flick of the tail! This is the nature of the

Massage improves flexibility, range of motion, and blood circulation and ultimately offers pain relief.

AMTIL (Animal Massage & Therapies)

Founded in 1998, AMTIL was created for the purpose of making the benefits of massage and other holistic approaches to animal health as widely available to companion animals as possible. The organization's website provides up-to-date information on all the therapies available for animals, including a directory of free listings and website links for practitioners of animal massage, acupressure, Reiki/energy work, herbal therapy, magnetic therapy, aromatherapy, color therapy, animal communication, flower essence therapy, homeopathy, and other modalities. You can visit its website at www.amtil.com.

beast. Always remember that dogs have masters and cats have staff.

TREATMENT

As I have already mentioned, every pet therapist has his own style, but many like to start each session with passive touch. This means simply resting their hands on the animal without applying any pressure at all. This initial touching practice helps create a comforting bond and establish a feeling of trust. At the same time, the soothing warmth from the therapist's hands allows the animal to relax and works on the circulation, making the muscle tissue softer and easier to work with in the following stages of the treatment. Some therapists continue to keep one hand on the pet at regular intervals throughout the session so that the low vibrations achieved from this light touch continue to allow energy to flow through the body.

When the cat is relaxed and obviously a willing participant, the therapist will begin long, slow effleurage movements to warm up the area. This gets the blood flowing. Sometimes a session will consist only of these long, gliding strokes. But if the cat is willing, the therapist will then engage in petrissage movements, drawing small concentric circles and gently rocking his hands from side to side to relax areas of muscle that are tight. This can be a very deep technique because as each layer of muscle opens, the therapist can attempt to work on the next one, all the way down to the bone. Deep muscle penetration acquired through these light pressure movements improves flexibility, range of motion, and blood circulation and ultimately offers pain relief. It's important to note that it is in no way painful, nor will it hurt your feline.

No pet massage session is choreographed movement by movement, and no two treatments will ever be the same. Ideally, therapists like to start around the face and the neck area because this region can hold a lot of tension; cats are usually more accepting of being touched in this area first. Next, they like to work down the chest and a front leg, along the back and down a back leg, along the tail, and then repeat the routine on the other side.

FINDING A PET MASSAGE THERAPIST

Unfortunately, there is no single controlling body that licenses pet massage therapists countrywide, so word of mouth is probably the best way of finding a therapist in your area. Also, check with your veterinarian to find out whether he has a working arrangement with someone he trusts.

Don't overlook your local pet boutique. Many forward-thinking boutique owners regularly invite massage therapists to work in-store to introduce their customers to the benefits of such a lifestyle treatment. They often hold demonstrations, too. It's an excellent idea to find out more about it firsthand and possibly book an initial consultation if you are confident about their expertise.

POPULAR PET MASSAGE AND HEALING TECHNIQUES

As I have already mentioned, there are various kinds of massage and healing therapies for pets out there. Pet therapists blend and borrow techniques and add their own interpretations. Here are summaries of the more popular modalities.

ACUPUNCTURE

This age-old healing technique has its roots in both China and India. In recent times, it's become very popular for both people and their pets. During treatment, a variety of small needles and sometimes a low-power laser are used to stimulate the acupuncture points on the body.

Acupuncture corrects the imbalances of energy known as qi (pronounced chee) within the body and unblocks obstructions in energy flow, thus allowing the qi to flow freely again and the body to heal itself. Along with the free-flowing energy, endorphins are released into the system, which helps reduce sensitivity to pain and stress.

Acupuncture is primarily used on pets to treat joint and muscular problems, but it is also said to aid pets being treated for cancer with chemotherapy. It's also an accepted form of treatment for respiratory problems such as chronic

Various kinds of massage and healing therapies used for people are also available for pets. For example, acupuncture is primarily used on pets to treat joint and muscular problems.

asthma and is used to stimulate the immune system to treat such diseases as feline leukemia and feline immunodeficiency virus.

Because this technique requires practitioners to have some detailed physiological knowledge of anatomy, it's usually practiced by veterinary acupuncturists or pet therapists who are also licensed veterinary technicians or who have some kind of medical background. Ask for credentials before making an appointment.

Pet massage therapists take cues from the animals themselves to see what they will tolerate and enjoy.

ACUPRESSURE

Acupressure is best described as acupuncture without needles. It works on the same principle but instead of needles or lasers, practitioners use finger pressure on specific points on the body. These pressure points are situated on channels, or meridians, along which the body's energy flows. Many pet therapists incorporate this modality into their general massage routine.

SHIATSU

Shiatsu is a Japanese form of massage therapy that's very similar to acupressure. In fact, the word means "finger pressure." The Shiatsu therapist usually applies pressure using his thumbs, although some may also use their fingers, palms, and even elbows to apply the required pressure to allow energy to flow freely. Often, some gentle massage is performed to the soft tissue areas around these meridians, as well as some gentle stretching movements.

REIKI

This form of healing also originated in Japan. The word "reiki" means universal life energy. By placing his hands on strategic points of the body, the therapist acts as a conduit by channeling the healing energy from himself directly to his pet patient.

TUINA

Tuina is a Chinese hands-on technique similar to Reiki. Apart from laying his hands on certain parts of the body, the therapist sometimes uses certain rolling or kneading movements to get the energy to flow. The word "tuina" (pronounced twee-nah) actually means push-grasp in Chinese.

This therapy also incorporates certain massage movements and acupressure techniques to help restore balance to the body and allow energy to flow freely once again, helping the body heal itself.

ESALEN MASSAGE
Apart from balancing the energy flow through the body, this technique also calls for gentle rocking movements, some passive joint exercises, and kneading movements to more deeply penetrate muscles and joints. These movements relieve pain and increase mobility in specific muscles and joints.

HOT STONE MASSAGE
Heated stones placed on the body provide gentle pain relief, and because the method is very relaxing, it simultaneously reduces stress levels. Practitioners of this treatment usually use river stones or lava rocks.

MASSAGE WITH THAI HEATED HERBAL COMPRESSES
Thai massage itself is not a therapy that applies to cats because it's best described as an interactive therapy that uses passive stretching and applied pressure to various parts of the body. It's a combination of acupressure, shiatsu, and yoga positions in which the masseur uses his thumbs, hands, and feet to achieve the desired effect. (And that includes walking on your back!) However, many pet therapists do use traditional Thai herbal compresses in their massage routines. Heated herbal compresses are excellent for sore or pulled muscles and ligaments, back pain, arthritis, and even stress and anxiety disorders. Typical ingredients include cassumunar ginger, lemongrass, kaffir lime leaves, eucalyptus, and sometimes camphor crystals. Together they are placed in a muslin cloth and then gently heated in a steamer or microwave. The compress is held in place for several minutes and is often used to end a pet massage therapy session.

TELLINGTON TOUCH
Tellington Touch therapy is a health and

Learning Pet Massage
There are many accredited pet massage schools around the country that offer workshops to make pet parents better informed about the basics. In fact, pet massage master W. Bruce Bregenzer says that it's possible to master the three basic pet massage techniques—passive touch, effleurage and petrissage—in a three-hour workshop.

Naturally, as with anything else, practice makes purrfect. But at least you will be able to give your fur kid a home petting session that's more than simply a bonding experience.

behavioral therapy that was especially designed for pets by horsewoman Linda Tellington-Jones. It was first used on horses in the 1970s as a system of animal training, healing, and communication.

The technique depends solely on the power of touch and doesn't involve any traditional massage movements or acupressure. The therapist uses circular finger and hand movements all over the body to relax the animal and thus reduce stress and any fears she may have. In cats, it's often recommended to treat extreme shyness, fear, and resistance to grooming, as well as to deal with excitability and nervous behavior. Although initially considered an animal therapy, these days health care professionals use it on people to reduce stress and anxiety, particularly after an illness.

THE DIY SUPERLATIVE PETTING SESSION

As we have already established, there's a lot you can do beyond just stroking your cat that can turn patting her into a superlative petting session equated with a body massage.

My cats aren't shy about coming to ask for a massage. And it doesn't matter if I'm busy with something else!

Fudge, my green-eyed beauty, can be fast asleep on the couch, but the moment I go to a particular kitchen counter, her kitty radar alerts her that if she gets there quickly, she will get a head rub and a gentle massage at the base of her tail. She controls the session. When she feels that she has had enough massaging around her ears and neck area, she moves down the counter so that my hand is positioned on her lower back. And just to make sure that I'm getting the message, she arches her back and flicks her tail in my face as a signal to work my fingers at the base of her tail. I oblige, of course. This is our standard kitchen counter routine. Now when she wants her ears scratched and the tips gently massaged, she will jump up on my desk in the office and stand in front of my computer screen so that I can't type, forcing me to attend to her instead. She sits and blinks dreamily. I know when she's had enough because she gets up and head-butts the computer monitor as a way of saying "thank you," and then she jumps off.

Cali, my 17-year-old calico, has her own massage routine. She waits until I get into bed at night and switch off the light. Then, like clockwork, she climbs up her pet steps onto the bed and plops down to share my pillow. This is her personal time for a rubdown. I try to follow Bregenzer's body pattern and start with her head and neck and then gently use long, stroking motions down her back, legs, and tail. Cali turns around when she wants the other side done. I get sheer enjoyment out of listening to her; she rumbles like an old Model T Ford. And when she's had enough, she'll grab my hand with both her paws and force me to stop.

Here are some massage/stroking routines that my cats have taught me. No doubt your cat has taught them to you, too. I bet you never really considered them to be do-it-yourself pet massage sessions before, did you?

EAR RINGS

Take your index finger and trace feather-light circles around the ear, letting your finger just touch the tips of the fur. There is a slight indented area below the opening of the ear. Take your index finger and gently massage this spot in a circular motion. Repeat on the other ear. Next, using two fingers, lightly massage the head. Start on the bridge of the nose, work on the top of the head between the ears, and finish at the back of the head, just above the collar.

On a purr scale of one to five, this should induce a five rating.

THE CHIN-CHIN

I don't believe there's a cat on the planet who doesn't like being stroked under the chin. My cats like me to start on the bottom lip and work down the neck. Often, they will butt my hand to make me stroke the top lip area, too.

On a purr scale of one to five, this should induce a five rating.

THE CHEEKY-CHEEK

Version One: Face your cat and cup your hands on either side of her face, with her chin resting where the palms of your hands meet. Gently vibrate your hands with a slight rocking motion. Mmm...good.

Version Two: Put your cat on your lap, or if she is lying on the floor, get down on your knees behind her. Take both hands and stroke her cheeks in slow, sweeping movements, starting on either side of her nose and ending up at the back of her head. Mmm...very good.

Version Three: Cup your cat's chin in your left hand and use two fingers to gently trace the bridge of her nose. Mmm...wonderful.

On a purr scale of one to five, all three movements should induce a five rating.

If your cat is unable to exercise due to injury or old age, you can stimulate circulation and healing as well as help her joints and muscles stay supple by flexing and massaging them everyday.

WHISKERS AWAY

Gently massage the area at the base of the whiskers. Some cats will even let you stroke the whiskers, closing their eyes in deep contentment.

On a purr scale of one to five, you guessed it—it's a five!

PAW-PRINT PURRS

Your cat needs to be lying down and very relaxed. Pick up a front paw, hold it, and gently massage the top of the foot. Next, apply gentle pressure to the paw pads and gently press each toe, allowing kitty a gentle stretching movement. If your fur kid will allow you to do this, you should have no trouble manicuring her toes at the end of one of these sessions.

On a purr scale of one to five, it's a five if you simply massage and a zero if you con her into allowing you to clip her toenails.

THE BIG BACK PURR

There isn't a cat on the planet who doesn't enjoy letting you run your hands down her back in long, slow movements. After that, you can work your way down the back on either side of the spine with gentle kneading movements. Finally, rub the area at the base of the tail. More than likely, kitty will arch her back and twist around, guiding your hand before flopping down flat wherever she is and purring heavily.

On a purr scale of one to five, this one is definitely a five.

THE TAIL END

My cat Fudge taught me this one. She loves to jump up on a counter or on my desk and stick her tail in my face. She wants me to stroke her tail from the base to the tip several times and then very, very gently, give it a tug, raising her back feet just a couple millimeters off the floor. Remember, very gently does it. This will always bring her back for more.

On a purr scale of one to five, this is a five.

THE CAT'S FIVE-STAR MEOW

You may have noticed that all the purr ratings rank a five. Of course! After all, your cat invented these routines by nuzzling and indicating where to rub and roll next. Cats are very good teachers, and once you've mastered the techniques they've taught you, high-volume purring is nothing more than the highest form of praise for your accomplishments. Let's face it: If you are struggling with a technique, your cat will instantly show her dissatisfaction by pushing away from you and leaving. Cats are far too busy to stick around while you fumble. They have other things to do, such as manicure their toes.

But all jokes aside, most cats respond warmly to the power of touch, and generally speaking, you can really do no wrong.

Tools of the Trade

Pet therapists use their hands to effleurage the back and sides of the body. But there's no reason why you can't use a cotton mitt or a special massage glove with rubber nodules to give your fur kid an all-over body rub, too.

My favorite massage tool is a cat-shaped comb with long rubber teeth that gently massages the skin and simultaneously combs the fur. And as an added bonus, it magnetically (and miraculously) attracts loose hair at the same time. Cats love the feel of it all over their bodies and will usually allow you to work on tender tummy areas, too.

Perhaps the most sophisticated gadget for home use is a special battery-operated pet vibrating massage roller. It's extremely silent, which means that most cats will tolerate it even on the top of their heads and under the chin. It has two speeds, allowing you to control the gentle vibrations as you move the roller slowly from head to tail, giving kitty a truly relaxing massage. They are usually sold in pet product catalogs and are often stocked by online pet stores.

Chapter Ten

The Purrfect Figure

Obesity among children is a growing problem in America, and sadly, it's become an issue we face with our feline fur kids, too. It is an unfortunate tradeoff for the safety and security of an indoor lifestyle. Cats need a proper diet combined with daily exercise, and being restricted indoors means that some may be tempted to become couch potatoes. So it's up to responsible pet parents to see that kitty keeps her purrfect figure.

*B*ut how do you know if your feline is purrfectly fit? Apart from popping her on a scale, the best way to judge if she needs to watch her weight is to do a regular "body check." If you can't feel your fur kid's ribs or she's looking a little spherical, it's time to take action. As with humans, there's no mystery here: Proper diet, which must provide appropriate feline nutrition, and exercise are all that is required to maintain good health and weight.

PROPER FELINE NUTRITION

To feed your finicky feline a healthy diet, you must know something about a cat's nutritional needs. Cats are carnivores, so they require a diet that primarily consists of meat. When fending for themselves in the wild, cats will catch a bird or mouse and consume almost all of it. The meat and internal organs provide essential proteins, vitamins, and minerals, while the bones and feathers are a source of fiber. The prey's stomach contents provide the small amount of vegetable matter that cats need. In their natural habitat, cats know how to eat properly.

Being aware of this, pet food manufacturers have studied the nutritional requirements that domestic house cats require to maintain good health. A high-quality commercial food containing the right amounts of proteins, fats, vitamins, and minerals will supply your feline with a daily balanced diet. The most important factors to keep in mind when selecting a food is that it should be a good-quality brand and contain all the necessary nutrients.

Also important to consider is that kittens and adult cats have different feeding requirements, so you must provide your pet with a balanced and healthy diet for her life stage. Growing kittens need two to three times more calories than adult and senior cats. They also require more fats, proteins, vitamins, and taurine in their diet while they are developing. Adult cats don't need the high-calorie food that kittens do, and feeding them this food will make them fat. In addition to the "regular" types of cat foods on the market, there are many specialty formulas available for adults. Pet food manufacturers have created specialty foods for overweight cats, senior cats, and even cats with urinary tract problems, dental problems, hairballs, and more. So if do your homework, your cat will be fit and trim.

TUBBY TABBIES: COUNTING THE KIBBLE

Now let's get back to keeping that purrfect figure. As with humans, being overweight can lead to major health problems for your feline, such as diabetes and liver disease. It also exacerbates arthritis. It's up to you to watch what goes into your kitty's food bowl. If you feel guilty that the bowl looks a tad too empty when you fill it at mealtimes, simply buy a smaller bowl!

Again, remember that cats are carnivores and need their daily intake of protein. They can't thrive on a vegetarian diet of zucchini and chewy mushrooms, even if you can. Further, don't ever let your cat con you into believing that she can diet by existing solely on the same kind of canned tuna that you love to mix with mayonnaise and spread on bread. This type of meal doesn't contain a balanced selection of nutrients.

And it's not only Garfield who loves lasagna. For some reason, cats seem to like foods that aren't good for them. (Sound familiar?) For example, most cats like a tomato-based sauce and will do anything to distract your attention so that they can climb on the table and lick your plate clean after you've eaten your spaghetti bolognaise. While the tomato-based sauce is okay as an occasional "lick treat" (if you haven't added sugar), the pasta part is definitely a no-no for svelte feline figures and good health.

Proper diet and exercise are all that is required to maintain your feline's good health and weight.

Remember that even if your cat does need to watch her weight, you cannot compromise her nutritional intake. Unfortunately, there is no Jenny Craig diet program for cats. Don't embark on any major changes without discussing a personalized weight-loss program with your veterinarian because a sudden drastic reduction in calories can induce health problems such as hepatic lipidosis, a life-threatening liver condition. At the least, it may cause an uncomfortable digestive upset. Your veterinarian will probably suggest a prescriptive calorie-controlled diet for your tubby tabby. This is an excellent choice because veterinary-prescribed calorie-controlled diets compensate by containing sufficient fatty acids to keep kitty's coat soft and silky and to stop her skin from flaking. And of course, they will promote her general good health.

However, having said this, cats occasionally need a little help with their diet in the form of additional vitamins and minerals.

DIET BOOSTERS

Generally, if your cat is fed a proper and balanced diet, she should not require calorie control or vitamin supplements. However, there are a few instances in which she may benefit from or require additional supplementation, such as when she is on a restricted diet, during pregnancy or illness, or if you feed a home-cooked diet. Always check with your vet before giving her supplements to ensure that she is getting the right ones in the correct dosage to meet her needs. Adding extra vitamins to her diet can be dangerous if you don't do so knowledgeably.

If you are instructed to offer a well-balanced multivitamin, it will contain the following ingredients:

- calcium ascorbate
- cellulose
- copper sulfate
- dicalcium phosphate
- dl-alpha tocopheryl acetate
- ferrous fumarate
- gelatin
- magnesium silicate
- magnesium stearate
- manganese sulfate

- niacinamide
- potassium chloride
- potassium iodide
- pyridoxine hydrochloride
- riboflavin
- safflower oil powder
- thiamine mononitrate
- vitamin B supplement
- vitamin D3 supplement
- zinc oxide

Before you give in to a defeatist attitude by saying "My cat will never take those," give her a chance to try. She may very well surprise you, even if she's a drama queen when it comes to taking vet-prescribed medications.

Many multivitamins are very palatable to cats. If kitty is not keen on crunching them whole, you can crush them and sprinkle them into food. The same applies to capsules. Open them and sprinkle, or alternatively, wrap them in pill poppers—that wonderful invention with the consistency of cookie dough.

My cats have always preferred dry food. Before I discovered pill poppers, I would always crush or sprinkle their pills into a spoon of kitty tuna, which was hardly ever rejected. Bottom line: Where there is a will, there's a way to get a cat to take her vitamins or any other medication, for that matter.

Obesity can lead to many health problems. If your cat is overweight, switch to scheduled feedings so that you can control what she eats.

CATCH THOSE CRAVINGS

You know what it's like when you diet—you crave treats. Your fur kid isn't any different, but be careful how you indulge her. If you give her commercial treats, read the label carefully and avoid anything high in fat. At long last the media have woken up and are pointing out that corn syrup and fructose are bad for humans; they're also bad for our pets, so try to avoid anything that contains corn syrup. Fortunately, there is no shortage of treats on the market, allowing you to pick and choose to ensure that your kitty isn't indulging in unnecessary calories.

Also, stay away from human treats. Chocolate, as every cat lover knows, is highly poisonous. And she doesn't need ice cream, even if she looks cute licking it from a cone. It's an obvious no-no to feed your cat human food for several reasons. Apart from the weight-gaining aspect, certain foods are toxic to cats or simply bad for them. For starters, you are not doing your cat any nutritional favors by feeding her large quantities of human-grade tuna because it lacks the correct vitamins and minerals to maintain a balanced diet.

It may be cute to see kitty investigating your mug of steaming hot chocolate with whipped cream on top, but chocolate, even in this form, is toxic to felines, along with tea, coffee, and alcoholic beverages. Also, stay away from onions in any form, baby foods (many of them contain onion powder), mushrooms, and potatoes. Salt and sugar are on the "no list," along with raw eggs and even a diet of raw fish because it can result in a vitamin B deficiency and cause both loss of appetite and even seizures.

However, one snack you can share together is popcorn made in a microwave oven. Just hold the butter and salt. Also, if your cat enjoys a particular canned food, try cutting it up into small squares and baking it in the oven at 350°F (177°C) until crispy, and store it in an airtight container. It makes a great feline snack between mealtimes.

Cats don't make good exercise buddies the way dogs do because they are not inclined to go romping after you as you go power walking or cycling. But there's nothing to stop you from being diet buddies and watching your weight together. Keep a food diary for both of you, and track your

Weighing In

Cats typically weigh between 5.5 and 16 lbs (2.5 to 7 kg). Some of the bigger breeds, such as the Maine Coon, can weigh in at around 25 lbs (11 kg). Just as with humans, maintaining a healthy weight is necessary to overall well-being and longevity. Remember, obesity is a killer, so watch what your fur kid eats. Many veterinarians suggest a diet that consists of both wet and dry food, but your best defense is to keep close tabs on how much your cat is eating and to remove food bowls after each feeding so that she can't overindulge. Also, don't give in to her pleadings for second helpings, and limit those treats—they're packed with calories.

weight loss. Keep in mind that cats lose weight at a very slow rate. A reduction of 1 pound (0.5 kg) on the scale is the equivalent of a human shedding 7 pounds (3.2 kg).

HEALTHY SNACKS: KITTY SALAD BARS

Just as pet parents like a little spice in their lives, their fur kids would also certainly enjoy an enticing addition to their daily meals. And who doesn't like an occasional tasty snack? There's no question that given the opportunity, most cats love to nibble on greenery and will consider anything from lush tropical houseplants to colorful floral accents a feline salad bar. But because there are so many plants that are toxic to cats, there's usually a negative spin put on plant nibbling.

But here's the good news: There's in fact a long and little-publicized list of nontoxic plants and flowers that your cat can snack on quite safely. They can be cultivated both indoors and outside on feline-secured balconies and patios.

GROWING EDIBLE GARDENS

Cats are particularly fond of the taste of different grasses. And although they thrive best on a protein-based diet and are obligate carnivores, they should be allowed to eat some greens like a side salad along with the main meal. After all, cats in the wild do this, so there's no reason that your domestic kitty shouldn't indulge as well.

Most cat parents are unaware that lots of very common and popular decorative houseplants such as orchids, African violets, bamboo palms, and various ferns are on the cat-safe list. Many common garden flowers such as zinnias and alyssum and herbs such as parsley, sage, thyme, and chickweed also make delicious edible feline snacks.

I'd like to dispel the old wives' tale that cats ingest greenery to deliberately induce vomiting. Cats are in fact very practical creatures and far too conscious of their self-image to ever be considered bulimic! When the foliage they've been snacking on is particularly hard to digest, they simply throw it up. There's no ulterior motive.

So if you've been playing it safe and only providing your fur kid with a little tub of kitty grass next to her food bowl, now is the time to give her a feline culinary adventure and grow a container of specially selected edibles for her to munch.

Both the ASPCA's Animal Poison Control Center and the Cat Fanciers' Association (CFA) publish comprehensive lists of nontoxic edible plants on their respective websites. My cats, especially Cali, have taste tested many of them and have given them the two-paws-up munch approval rating. You can check these out at www.aspca.org and www.cfa.org.

POTS AND PLANTERS

You don't have to have a green thumb to grow a feline-friendly container of yummy plants for your

Kitty Greens

Spoil your cat by buying a special kitty greens kit that comes neatly packaged in a compact wood planter. It includes four seed compartments containing oats, wheat, rye, and barley, plus a water-absorbing growing medium and liners. The seeds sprout quickly and are ready to nibble on within days. Because your cat may favor certain plants over others, you may find yourself replacing her favorites on a regular basis. Or you can create your own edible garden. Here are two great suggestions:

The Kitty Grass Salad Bar (for outdoors—full sun)

Requirements: 6-inch (15-cm) stack pot consisting of 4 pots; 1 cu ft (28 l) tropical potting soil (contains 60% peat moss, 30% pumice, 10% sand) This will be enough soil for two planters of this size. Stack pot planters come in different sizes and are usually stocked by independent nurseries. Buy bigger plants for bigger pots.

Plants:
1. 4-inch (10-cm) *Pennisetum* (Eaton canyon grass)
2. 4-inch (10-cm) *Scirpus cernuus* (fiber-optic grass)
3. 4-inch (10-cm) Carex "Evergold" (Japanese clumping grass)
4. 4-inch (10-cm) *Helictotrichon sempervirens* (blue oat grass)

Plant according to the plant map.

The Kitty Zen Garden (for indoors)

Requirements: A fiberglass or plastic Zen-styled rectangular planter; 1 cu ft (28 l) tropical potting soil (contains 60% peat moss, 30% pumice, 10% sand); 1 bag river rocks for decoration.

Plants:
1. 4-inch (10-cm) yellow oncidium orchid
2. 6-inch (15-cm) (parlor palm)
3. 4-inch (10-cm) *Avena sativa* (cat oat grass)
4. 4-inch (10-cm) *Pellaea rotundifolia* (button fern)
5. 4-inch (10-cm) African violet (any color)

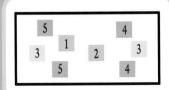

Plant according to the plant map.

cat to enjoy. You just need to gather up the right materials. When it comes to pots and planters, you can select anything that has visual appeal, will blend well with your home decor, or make a great decorative accent on an enclosed outdoor area.

Make sure that the planter has good drainage, and if the container you select doesn't have any drainage holes, ask the nursery to drill some for you. It's always advisable to place a saucer underneath the planter to prevent water from staining the surface on which the planter is standing. A cork mat is an excellent choice. For large outdoor containers, consider purchasing special decorative pot feet (obtainable from all nurseries and plant stores) to raise the planter sufficiently off the ground to prevent this problem.

If you are planning to take indoor planters outside to water them, make sure that you are able to lift them once they've been planted. Lightweight plastic or fiberglass planters that resemble intricate cement or ceramic materials are a great option.

SOIL MIX AND FERTILIZERS

For indoor planters, a mixture of peat moss, pumice, and sand is best. Some nurseries sell it prepackaged, so ask. Sand is an important component for drainage. Plants that enjoy shade usually do well in an acid mix made up of equal parts of peat moss and pumice. Once again, check to see if you can buy it premixed. The same soil mixes can be used for outdoor planters, too.

Cats love to nibble on greenery, so make sure the houseplants you keep are nontoxic to your kitty.

PREPARING THE PLANTER

Once you have purchased all the necessary materials, you're ready to create your feline's fantasy garden.

Fill your planter with soil, and dig a hole slightly bigger than the plant you are positioning. Put the plant in the hole, then gently pack the surrounding soil to keep it in place. Start with the larger plants and fill in with the smaller ones.

Plants bought from nurseries and other reputable plant outlets are planted in good soil containing fertilizers, so wait two to four weeks before fertilizing them yourself. Thereafter, make a note to do it every eight weeks. Because you are planting for pets, use a liquid organic fertilizer made from either seaweed or a fish extract. Stay away from chemical-based products and snail and slug baits, which are highly poisonous to animals.

WATER REQUIREMENTS

When planting an indoor pot containing various plants, you must ensure that they have adequate water requirements. Your watering program will depend on the amount of light, humidity, and air circulation in the area in which the container stands.

Let temperature dictate watering habits. At temperatures around 70°F (24°C), water twice a week. In climates where the temperature rises above 85°F (29°C), water every other day. In cold weather, water once a week.

AQUA GARDENS

If you don't have space for a large container, your cat may enjoy an aqua garden of hydroponically grown cat grass. These garden units attach to the side of a drinking fountain and contain seedpods that can be replaced from time to time. The seeds actually germinate in the water of the fountain within two to three days, giving kitty a fresh, edible snack. They are available from most pet stores. Your cat will thank you for always having fresh greens on tap—so to speak!

POISONOUS PLANT ACCIDENTS

The ASPCA's Animal Poison Control Center receives several hundred calls a year from distressed pet owners whose pets have eaten highly toxic plants, especially lilies. Familiarize yourself with these plants, and never keep them in your home or outdoors. The toxins in poisonous plants have varied effects on cats, ranging from a skin rash to vomiting and diarrhea. Nibbling on the wrong plants can even cause convulsions resulting in a coma, kidney failure, and death.

If your cat nibbles on the wrong thing, she is going to need urgent medical attention. Rush her to your veterinarian or nearest pet emergency room, and take a sample of the plant with you, or call the ASPCA Animal Poison Control Center at 1-888-426-4435. A fee may be charged to your credit card.

The Top Ten Most Poisonous Plants

Here is the ASPCA's list of the ten most common poisonous plants encountered by pets.

- ❖ **Lilies.** All lilies are very popular indoor plants, especially around Easter. As beautiful as they are, they are highly toxic to cats and can cause severe kidney damage.

- **Sago Palm.** This plant can potentially produce vomiting, diarrhea, depression, seizures, and liver failure. All parts of the plant are poisonous, but the seeds, or "nuts," contain the largest amount of toxins.
- **Tulip/Narcissus.** The bulb portions of these plants contain toxins that can cause intense gastrointestinal irritation, drooling, loss of appetite, central nervous system depression, convulsions, and cardiac abnormalities.
- **Azalea/Rhododendron.** This plant contains substances known as grayanotoxins, which can produce vomiting, drooling, diarrhea, weakness, and central nervous system depression in animals. Severe azalea poisoning could ultimately lead to coma and death from collapse of the cardiovascular system.
- **Cyclamen.** This plant contains cyclamine; the highest concentration of this toxic component is typically located in the tuber (root) portion of the plant. If consumed, it can produce significant gastrointestinal irritation, including intense vomiting. Fatalities have also been reported in some cases.
- **Marijuana.** Ingesting this plant in any form can result in central nervous system depression, as well as vomiting, diarrhea, vocalization, drooling, increased heart rate, and even seizures or coma.
- **Oleander.** All parts of the oleander plant are considered to be toxic because they contain cardiac glycosides that have the potential to cause serious effects. These include gastrointestinal tract irritation, abnormal heart function, a significant drop in body temperature (hypothermia), and even death.
- **Castor Bean.** The poisonous principle in this plant is ricin, a highly toxic protein that can produce severe abdominal pain, drooling, vomiting, diarrhea, excessive thirst, weakness, and loss of appetite. In severe cases, dehydration, muscle twitching, tremors, seizures, coma, and death can occur.
- **Kalanchoe.** This plant can cause gastrointestinal irritation and also seriously affect cardiac rhythm and heart rate.
- **Yew.** This plant contains taxine, which affects the central nervous system, causing trembling, lack of coordination, and breathing difficulties, as well as significant gastrointestinal irritation and cardiac failure, which can result in death.

DIET PILLS AND APPETITE SUPPRESSANTS

While the US Food and Drug Administration (FDA) has approved a weight-loss drug for dogs, there is nothing currently on the market for cats. And no, liposuction is not a safe alternative to body sculpt a svelte feline form, as previously discussed. However, there are some herbal tablets

Always get your vet's approval before beginning your cat's weight-loss program.

on the market that contain garcinia cambogia, which is a natural appetite suppressant and is said to slow down the production and storage of fat. These tablets are available from holistic pet food stores and online stores.

Simply remember that with any weight-loss program, perseverance and patience are key words. Also, your vet should give it his stamp of approval.

LOOK YOUNG, STAY YOUNG

If you feel good, you often look good. The one area in which cats have both dogs and humans beat is in the looks department. They never seem to age visibly. Going gray isn't a typical feline problem; they somehow manage to look as glamorous at 9 months old as they do at 9 years and even as 19-year-old seniors.

Cats show their age by sometimes shrinking in size, and of course, in the way they walk. They definitely become less mobile and are not able to jump great heights in later years. Sometimes it's just stiff joints from old age, but more often than not, the problem is exacerbated by arthritis.

Officially, cats register as seniors from the age of seven. That's a good time to start considering adding nutraceuticals such as glucosamine and chondroitin to their daily diet, before the possible onset of osteoarthritis.

NUTRACEUTICALS—THE NEW BUZZWORD

A nutraceutical as defined by Dr. Stephen DeFelice, founder and chairman of the Foundation for Innovation in Medicine (FIM) who coined the word in the 1990s, is "any substance that is a food or a part of a food and provides medical or health benefits, including the prevention and treatment of disease."

Glucosamine and chondroitin tablets are classified as nutraceuticals. Studies have shown that glucosamine, a 2-amino derivative of glucose, and chondroitin, which is found in animal cartilage, including whale and shark cartilage, have a therapeutic effect on joint and cartilage problems in both cats and dogs.

When my calico cat California was 15 years old, she pulled a ligament in her hind leg. The vet said that she would have been in worse trouble if she had not been taking glucosamine and chondroitin tablets for a number of years. (Pssst…if you are over 40, chances are it will be good for you, too!)

Another popular nutraceutical for cats is an omega-3 fatty acid supplement derived from fish oil. Fatty acids are known to improve the quality of cat fur and add sheen.

Because the feline health and beauty industry mirrors the human health and beauty industry so closely, I have found that pet parents who add nutraceuticals to their own daily food intake are more likely to consider which supplements may be beneficial to their pets, too.

It's important to note that nutraceuticals are not regulated by the FDA. Consequently, while products may look the same, dosage and the quality may differ greatly. So read labels carefully, and don't try anything without taking advice from your veterinarian, who is aware of your feline's general health. He will also know what medications your fur kid is taking, which is important because some medicines should not be combined with supplements.

As far back as the 1920s, nutritionist Dr. Victor Lindlahr, who was a strong believer in the idea that food controls health, said, "Ninety percent of the diseases known to man are caused by cheap foodstuffs. You are what you eat." In the 1960s, Adelle Davis, a leading spokesperson for the organic food movement, also touted this phrase. These words still hold true today—and they apply to our cats, too!

To ensure your feline remains "purrfectly" fit, do a regular body check—
if you can't feel her ribs or she feels too thin, it's time to take action.

Chapter Eleven

Feline Fitness: Fun and Games

Not only is playtime a wonderful way to help kitty watch her weight and burn off the unwanted calories she may have consumed, but it also provides the mental stimulation and exercise she needs on a daily basis. This is especially important if your cat has taken to being a lazy lump or a grouch! Cats who don't get enough play or interaction with their owners can become bored, restless, or develop behavior problems—all good reasons to plan regular playdates with your fur kid.

*D*on't worry. I'm not talking about anything really strenuous—just 40 minutes a day of fun and games with a variety of cat toys. You can split your exercise games into two sessions or mini-workouts throughout the day. Not only does exercise burn fat and calories as it does in people, but it also helps maintain healthy joints and muscle mass. Playing games will also keep your kitty intellectually stimulated and mentally alert and hone her natural instincts, too.

And there are even more pluses. By getting involved in feline fun and games, you are spending real quality time together. What a great way to strengthen that wonderful emotional bond you share with your fur kid!

Exercise Monitor

One way to keep track of your cat's level of exercise is to buy a pet pedometer and attach it to her collar to occasionally keep tabs on her energy level. Don't leave it on permanently because it can be cumbersome around her neck. Of course, you also stand the chance of having her refuse to move at all the moment you put it on, thwarting your plans altogether!

FUN TOYS—AKA EXERCISE EQUIPMENT

Although cats can be very inventive and turn just about anything from a rolled-up sock to a shopping bag into a plaything, toy manufacturers have been honing their research skills and sharpening their design capabilities to come up with some really innovative ideas. The latest toys really do pique feline curiosity and take care of various emotional, instinctual, and physical requirements, such as the need to hunt, scratch, and interact with other felines in the household when their pet parents aren't around to be their official events coordinator.

By ensuring that your fur kid has plenty of toys and possibly her own cat tree or kitty condo play center to hang out in, she will also be less likely to be bored and thus less destructive around the house.

INTERACTIVE TOYS

Cat toys can be divided into two main categories: interactive toys that involve you as a feline playmate and those that will distract your kitty and keep her busy when she's home alone. Interactive toys are great because you get to spend quality time with your kitty—and you can be sure that she'll be expecting playtime every day once she realizes how much fun it can be. Interactive toys are widely available from all pet stores, pet boutiques, and pet catalogs and online stores.

WANDS AND FISHING FUN

Yes, cats in the wild really do fish!

Wands with furry or feathery things on the end or fishing rods with a toy dangling at the end of the line are cleverly constructed to hone feline hunting and fishing skills and should definitely be included in your feline's toy box.

Wands can sport a variety of materials, such as a furry tail or a length of stretch fabric that will "jump" when pounced upon and fly off in another direction. There are wands with feathers and bells that simulate a bird in flight and others that combine all these features. When playing together, make sure that you move the wand across and away from yourself to prevent your cat from accidentally clawing you. Fishing rods with a little catnip-filled fish on the end will also engage both of you in endless hours of amusement. But be sure not to hit your cat in the face or knock over any valuable ornaments when you cast the rod!

Cats see such toys as "lively" prey substitutes. When a toy wand or rod flies through the air and your cat swings around and follows it, pouncing on it and "killing" it, she will sometimes also do a backward flip using both front feet to trap her prey. When most doting pet parents see these actions, they simply think that their little furball is being inventive and very intelligent. But in fact, these antics are nothing more than instinctive hunting actions that a cat would perform in the wild.

Aside from honing her natural instincts, playtime provides your cat with necessary stimulation and exercise.

Cats have three different hunting patterns they use depending on what type of prey they are after. When hunting for mice, they stalk, pounce, and trap with their front feet and then bite. That's also what they do when you are trailing something along the ground. When you fling a wand into the air, simulating a flying object, they will follow through by leaping and swiping at it with both feet at once. Finally, if you leave something trailing on the ground, they will lie in wait as they would do if they were at the water's edge watching movement below the surface. In the real-life scenario,

Most indoor pet cats are understimulated and will best thrive by being kept entertained. Interesting toys and activities can keep your fur kid busy and happy while she's home alone.

when an unwary fish swims by, they will suddenly dip their paws into the water and slide them under the fish's body, flipping it out of the water and behind them. The fish is then stranded on the grass, and they will swing around and pounce on it. Cats practice these tactics all the time, especially when playing with balls or crumpled pieces of paper.

BALL GAMES

You can train your cat to bat a ball in your direction to initiate a game of catch. You'll need to buy them by the dozen because for some unknown reason, they tend to disappear around the house. (Your fur kid probably has a secret stash somewhere!) Fortunately, they're inexpensive toys.

Stock up on a variety of different ones. Some are made of a very soft rubber that allows a cat to hold them with her claws. Some have bells inside. Look for balls that chirp and make interesting noises and also for fabric-covered ones with feathers attached. The fabric allows a cat to grab them and toss them high in the air. And of course, you can make them "fly," too! Cats often love to play with a ball on their own, which allows you to get on with other things.

LASER TOYS

Laser toys are great because you can multitask, enjoy a cup of coffee, and possibly even read a book while commandeering a laser dot to fly around the room and shimmy across the floor. Many come with different heads so that you can exchange a red dot for a mouse-shaped one. Your feline is unlikely to notice the difference, but it will certainly make you feel more involved!

Lasers rev up a cat's prey drive, but be sure to let the beam rest in a spot long enough for her to pounce and try to capture her prey. Never get the beam in her eyes. Also, because laser play isn't really a fair game—after all, your cat will never catch anything—be sure that the next toy you bring out is one that she can actually capture and kick around with her paws.

MICE OF ALL SHAPES AND SIZES

No cat can resist little furry mice! Mice come in all shapes and sizes. Little ones with bells or rattles inside generate a lot of fun. Most cats usually bite them to pieces to "attack" the noise, so remove the remnants so that they aren't accidentally swallowed. Soft fabric mice usually contain a pouch that you can fill with catnip and constantly refresh to keep games stimulating and amusing. Some of them even have little wheels to help them scurry across the floor.

BATTERY-OPERATED TOYS

There's a huge selection of battery-operated toys designed to taunt feline curiosity. A battery-operated remote-controlled mouse will also have your feline darting all over the room. Some toys with wands move in various directions and can be enjoyed by more than one cat at a time. Some of these items are so sophisticated that they can be programmed to switch on and initiate play while you are out! Also look for battery-operated mice that travel on a track and items that fling out string and provide endless amusement.

TINY BUBBLES

Both cats and kids love bubbles, so let them play together. Ordinary bubbles will provide endless fun, but your cat will enjoy a special catnip bubble solution available from most pet stores even more.

HOME ALONE: SELF-PLAY AND DISTRACTION TOYS

Most indoor pet cats are understimulated and will thrive best by being kept entertained. Of course, the best feline enrichment is playing with you or another cat. But when that's not possible, interesting toys and activities can keep your fur kid busy and happy while she's home alone. Cats are highly intelligent and can become easily bored, so the operative word here is variety.

KITTY GYMS AND ACTIVITY CENTERS

Most easy-to-assemble kitty gyms offer cats a variety of on-tap entertainment and include a selection of items that spin, dangle, whirl, and twirl. Some have tassels with bells and balls, too. Certain designs are combined with a scratching pad or include toy birds on a spring device that move instantaneously at the touch of a swatting paw. Remove and replace any parts that look worn and torn so that your cat doesn't accidentally swallow something.

Rules of the Game

Remember to regularly rotate toys to keep feline interest piqued. And be careful which toys you leave out when you are not around because many can be potentially harmful if ingested or may even get wound around your cat's neck. Never leave your fur kid home alone with anything that dangles, such as string, stretch fabrics, or ribbons. Put small balls and cat toys with feathers out of reach when not in play, and during the festive seasons, don't give your cat access to Christmas tree tinsel and decorations. Clean out the toy box regularly and discard old toys.

PUZZLE GAMES

Puzzle games are guaranteed to provide endless hours of fun and games. They intellectually challenge your cat while allowing her to hunt and generally entertain herself. Some of the most stimulating include large square boxes with balls or toys that are trapped within the framework but move around powered by a feline paw. Another firm favorite is a wheel-shaped tunnel with a fast-moving ball that spins when batted. You can step up the intensity of the game by adding a few random treats that kitty will have to fish out with her paw to retrieve and enjoy.

TUNNELS AND BAGS OF FUN

Cats love tunnels and bags that they can climb into to play games of hide-and-seek with themselves or other felines in the family. Some toys resembling brown paper bags make a crinkly noise when moved. Others even have toys inside that move around to keep your cat intrigued. You can hide treats and other toys in there, too.

CAT WHEELS

If your cat enjoys going for walks but is thwarted by having to stay indoors during the cold, wet, or snowy winter months, you may want to consider investing in a cat wheel. It looks like a giant hamster wheel and is usually sold at cat shows or from specialist online feline-supply stores. Certain athletic and energetic breeds such as Bengals love spinning around in a wheel, and they are very popular form of exercise for show cats. You will never know if your cat will like it unless you try.

FELINE TREASURE HUNT

If you know that you're going to be out for a lengthy period, why not plan a treasure hunt to keep your cat entertained in your absence? Simply place some of her favorite toys and low-calorie treats in different hiding places around your home, and leave her to seek them out and have some fun.

HOMEMADE TOYS

Lots of household objects make great toys. The silver paper encasing a slab of chocolate is a fun lightweight ball. A cardboard box that your new computer came in can be transformed into a great playhouse. Giant paper shopping bags provide hours of fun (but be sure to cut the handles off so that kitty can't get them caught around her neck). Grab some unwanted shoelaces and nail them to a piece of wood. (A discarded broom handle cut to size will do.) You can hold the wood and let the shoelaces "dance," which will get your cat in the groove!

ENTERTAINMENT

Studies have shown that some cats do watch television. If you are not home, consider tuning in to a station such as Animal Planet or screen special cat videos. These videos can act as babysitters for your cat by capturing her attention with flying objects and noises of other animals and birds.

How to Play With Your Cat

While playing with your cat may appear to be a no-brainer, you need to be sure that you are doing it right. In order for it to be truly beneficial and satisfying for your fussy feline, it must stimulate her hunting instincts. This basically means that you need to be sure that she is able to catch the toy "prey" occasionally and have the opportunity to chew or scratch at it a bit. Otherwise, you will simply frustrate her, and she won't think the game is fun anymore. After all, it isn't any fun to play a game if you never win, is it?

When you move a toy around on the floor or on a pole or fishing line, do it in a way that resembles the natural movements of prey. Flop it around a bit like a wounded bird or pull it across the floor in erratic directions like a running mouse. Cats also find it fun and challenging when the toy is hidden behind or under something.

When you decide to stop playing, your cat may just walk away, but if she's still in need of activity slowly tone down the play by allowing your cat to catch the toy a few more times before quitting. Substituting another toy she can play with on her own is a good solution if she's still raring to go.

Make sure that your television is not easy to knock over or that your flat screen is firmly anchored to the wall—an overenthusiastic kitty may get carried away and launch herself at the screen.

AGILITY COMPETITIONS

Toys are fun but if your cat is a real extrovert, loves running, jumping, and climbing, and has crazy spurts rushing around at record speed, she may be a prime candidate to learn cat agility.

Cat agility is similar to dog agility and maybe even horse show jumping, for that matter. In agility trials, the animal has to go around a timed obstacle course. A target is used to lure the cat around the course (usually a stick with feathers on the end), so if your fur kid is already clicker trained, you are on your way.

In the last few years, this feline sporting activity has grown in popularity. Cat agility courses are often set up at cat shows, country fairs, adoption events, and sometimes even in pet stores. These events usually draw an enthusiastic crowd of both participants and onlookers.

WHO'S UP FOR THE COURSE?

The best part about this sport is that it's open to all cats. Your feline doesn't have to have an impressive pedigree or needn't have participated in a cat show to enjoy this pastime. Any feline starting as young as eight months old can be taught to enjoy this enriching activity; she just has to have lots of energy and be physically fit. Check with your veterinarian if you are considering signing her up for lessons—he can check for physical impediments that could be exacerbated by the endurance challenges involved.

The obstacle courses are designed with both feline safety and fun in mind and have great spectator appeal. There are different levels of competition, and cats can win titles at any level. There is never any pressure to advance to a higher level or to attempt something that is beyond your cat's physical capabilities. It's all about fun and games. Needless to say, it's also a great form of exercise to burn calories and keep your cat healthy and trim.

PRACTICE MAKES PURRFECT

To get your feline into shape for competition, it's easy to set up an agility course and practice at home. Most pet stores sell tunnels and other equipment, and you can design a course in any room of your house. Dining room chairs make great hurdles, and you can tie a hula hoop between two chairs at a particular height for your fur kid to jump through.

The secret is to practice every day. No doubt you won't even have to take your feather stick to lure her after a while because she'll be off and running on her own.

At home your cat will be in familiar surroundings, but when you take her to an event, it's a good idea to allow her to walk around the course alone first to orient herself. When she's comfortable in her surroundings, she will signal you by putting her tail up in a happy cat position, and you will know that she's ready to try to beat the clock. Some cats can rush around a course at the speed of lightning in seconds.

WHEN YOUR CAT HIRES A TRAINER—YOU!

There may be times when your kitty needs a little encouragement or help staying active. Although kittens often play so hard that they wear themselves out, overweight or senior cats may not have as much energy. Whether your cat is spunky or sedentary, regular, moderate exercise will help keep her joints limber and strong. It will strengthen and tone her muscles, maintain her at a proper weight, increase her energy level, help her sleep better, strengthen her cardiovascular system, and keep her internal organs strong and healthy. So get her moving!

COME ON! LET'S GO!: WALKING ON A LEASH

The first time you put a leash on a fully grown cat and say "Come on, let's go!" the chances are your kitty will lie down and refuse to budge. And if you do manage to coax her outside, she will undoubtedly charge under a bush and leave you searching amongst the foliage trying to work out how to extricate her. Simply put, cats don't take to walking on a leash the way ducks take to water. But if you begin a walking program from kittenhood, a cat can be trained to enjoy outings as part of her exercise routine. And cats of any age can partake!

Having the right harness relieves

As few as 10 to 15 minutes of exercise a day will bring positive results for your indoor kitty. Spending daily quality time playing with her will also strengthen the bond you share.

Exercise and the Senior Cat

Although you can't slow the march of time, you can slow some of its negative effects on your aging cat by keeping her as active as she can be for as long as possible. As your cat enters her senior years, she won't need as much activity as she did as a youngster or an adult, but she must do more than toddle to her food bowl. Unfortunately, some of her physical limitations may keep her from self-exercising as she used to do, so it's up to you to encourage her to move around a bit—and the best way to do that is to play with her. Just this amount of activity will boost her energy, keep her limber, keep her mind active, and help prevent the emotional shifts that all too often accompany old age. With a little bit of imagination, patience, and a simple toy, you can capture her interest as well as her heart.

part of the battle. Use one that fastens on top. A soft padded harness that's ostensibly made for a small dog will also be comfortable on a cat. Avoid designs that fasten under the tummy because there's no way your fur kid is going to lie on her back and let you fasten her in securely.

Going for regular walks is great feline exercise. Cats can be trained to go the distance and can make great walking companions. However, it's important to plan your route so that your chosen paths are not frequented by any dogs who may either charge your feline or come too close out of curiosity.

PURRLATES ANYONE?

As a writer, I am deskbound most of the day (and night). Consequently, I constantly suffer from neck and related shoulder and arm pains. And despite constant threats from my physical therapist that I should get up regularly and do some basic stretches, it never became routine until my cats stepped in and took control of the situation. They are constantly around me when I work. Cali likes to sleep on the pile of research papers at my feet, and Fudge likes to sit on my desk and watch the cursor on the computer screen. Occasionally, when she wants attention, she stands in front of the screen, blocking my view, and refuses to budge until I have played with her.

That's when I realized that I could combine some therapeutic stretches for myself and play with her at the same time. I have called the following exercises Sandy's Purrlates Workout. Although they won't have a huge calorie-burning effect on your feline, involving her in these gentle stretches means that she will be have to tense various muscles in her body to hold her balance. This can only be good for her, right? Gentle exercise is also good for seniors who may be physically challenged and unable to get the activity they need to stay healthy longer.

However, it goes without saying that if kitty is not a keen participant (and she may not be particularly willing if she is overweight), then drop it—the idea that is, not the cat! And remember, while these are adaptations of genuine exercises, there is nothing scientific here for your feline other than fun and getting to spend some quality time with you. Of course, be sure that you're both medically fit to try them.

Kiss and Tell

Sit upright in any chair and place your cat on your lap. Lock your fingers behind your head and hold your elbows out to the sides. Keeping your back as straight as possible, bend forward, stretching out your neck and shoulders, and try to kiss your cat on the top of her head. Repeat ten times. You will know that you are doing the exercise correctly when she begins to purr.

Uppurr Flex

This exercise stretches the upper trapezius. Sit upright with your cat on your lap. Gently grasp the side of your head with your left hand while reaching behind your back with the other hand. Tilt your head to the left until you feel a gentle stretch. Hold for 30 seconds. Repeat three times on each side, and remember to pet your cat before changing to the other side.

Neck Purrfect

To gently stretch your upper spine, hold your cat on your lap and gently massage her shoulders. Hold your head straight, and pull your chin back while keeping your eyes and chin level at all times. Hold each movement for two seconds and repeat ten times.

Chest and Shoulder Purrs

You can sit with your cat in your lap, but better still, stand and hold her around her waist and in front of you close to your chest. Maintain erect posture. Keeping your elbows close to your sides, roll your shoulder blades back in a circular movement. It's a gentle movement for kitty and gives your shoulders and chest a nice stretch. Repeat ten times. Don't expect any purrs on this one—your cat will just think that you're a little odd.

Lift One, Purr Two—Calf Raises

Sit upright with your feet next to one another on the floor. Keep your cat on your lap. Gently lift your heels off the floor, raising them up as far as they will go to get a nice stretch in your calves. Some cats are so relaxed that they don't move a muscle. But if you do it vigorously, kitty may have to tense up her tummy to hold on.

Pelvic Tilt and Purr

Lie flat on the floor with your knees bent and your feet close to your buttocks. Place your cat on your tummy. Pull in your abdominal muscles, and simultaneously lift your buttocks off the floor and squeeze—your buttocks, not the cat. This movement is purrfect to strengthen the lower back, abdominals, and the sacroiliac joint. Kitty will have to tense some muscles too to maintain balance and stay in place.

Rollovers

Lay on your back with your legs bent and curled up to your chest. Stretch your arms out on either side of you. Choose a cat toy on a wand that springs and jumps about as you wave it. Hold it in one hand. Place your cat next to you, and make sure that she engages in the movement of the toy. Now slowly swing your legs from side to side, and as you do so, flick the wand so that the toy jumps about and engages your cat's attention. She will keep running around you as you roll from side to side. This is for your abdominals and for kitty's pure enjoyment. Yes, it takes a bit of coordination. No doubt she will get bored and wander off and then you can concentrate and get some benefit from the exercise for yourself.

PARTY TRICKS—REALLY!

Not many cat parents are aware that teaching your cat to perform tricks qualifies as feline enrichment and fitness. It's very easy to train a cat to perform a repertoire of fun acts, from playing fetch and shaking paws to doing fun party tricks such as a high-five greeting or playing "Three Blind Mice" on the piano. Because you'll be out and about, why not show off your favorite feline by demonstrating her many talents?

The secret to turning kitty into an artiste is a simple positive reinforcement training technique called clicker training. Invented by behavioral scientist Karen Pryor to initially train dolphins, the technique is now widely used to train dogs and is equally successful on cats.

Teaching your fur kid to fetch on demand, shake paws, or dance in a circle definitely qualifies as feline enrichment because the actions are stimulating and fun for her to do, and once again, training goes a long way toward further cementing the wonderful relationship you share.

TARGET AND TREAT

Clicker training is nothing more than bargaining with your feline. You're telling your cat "If you perform this action, I will reward you with your favorite tuna treat or a play session with your special toy."

This training method revolves around using a marker or target such as a pencil or a rod to point and identify what you want your cat to do. You use a handheld clicker to "click" and tell her that she's done the right thing and is thus entitled to receive an instant reward.

Party Animal Fabulous!

Two party tricks that Karen Pryor has successfully taught thousands of cats to do to entertain an appreciative audience are the kitty high-five greeting and how to play "Three Blind Mice" on the piano. The latter can be taught on a regular piano or on a child's toy piano.

Kitty High Five

This trick is always a crowd pleaser.

❖ First, you'll need to train your cat to sit. Wait until she does it of her own accord, and then capture it by clicking and treating. Do this several times until she has figured it out. Make sure that she can repeat this in any room in the house, and then establish a cue so that she will learn to do it on command. It can be the word "sit," or you can use a simple hand gesture.

❖ To teach the high five "slap," wiggle your fingers and move your hand in front of your cat's paw on the ground. The moment she pats your fingers with her paw, click and treat.

❖ When she consistently pats your moving fingers, slowly raise your hand off the ground until it's up in the air aligned with your cat's shoulder height.

❖ When your cat raises her paw, put your hand in the path of the movement and click the instant the paw touches your hand.

❖ Next, move your hand slightly so your cat has to aim for your hand with her paw to get clicked.

❖ Finally, add the verbal cue "Gimme five" when you hold out your hand. Click and treat.

Piano Recital: "Three Blind Mice"

It's advisable to teach this feline piano recital over a two-day period.

Day One:

❖ Prepare about 20 very small, healthy treats. Place an empty plate on the piano bench. Lure your cat to the seat, click as she jumps up, and put a treat on the plate. If she stays on the bench, click and treat again. Repeat this process until she learns that she must remain on the bench. When she does this reliably, move on to the next step.

❖ Next, hold a treat over the keyboard. Click any movement toward the keyboard and any paw touch on the keys. When she does so, put a treat on the plate so that your cat must come down to the bench to eat and get back up to the keys to get clicked.

❖ Next, wait for your cat to move toward the keys or step on them without any help from you. Click any attempt, even if she just looks at the keys.

❖ When she is stepping on or pawing at the keys with confidence, click only for strong paw pats. Click any audible plinks and reward with extra food.

Day Two:

❖ Repeat the first steps done the day before. When your cat can make audible plinks on a regular basis, click and treat every second paw touch to build repeated sounds.

❖ Put small removable stickers or sticky notes on the piano keys Middle C, D, and E. Click only when your cat touches those keys.

❖ Pryor suggests continuing to click for repeated plinks over the next few days and especially for any right to left movement that follows the tune of the song.

❖ When your cat is hitting the notes E, D, and C in order, she is playing "Three Blind Mice"!

Applause, please! Kitty would prefer lots of treats to a bouquet of flowers, thank you.

GETTING STARTED

The idea is to shape each behavior by teaching your cat to touch the target (the stick) with her nose. If you hold the target close to her face, she will inevitably touch it by sniffing it. As your cat's nose is coming close to the target, "capture" the behavior by clicking it and immediately give her a treat. It's important to remember that every time you click, you *must* treat.

Practice your mechanical skills in front of a mirror before you even introduce your cat to a target. Hold the target and the clicker in the same hand. Put the target stick up to the mirror, and click when the stick touches the mirror. Instantly put a tiny bit of tuna from one dish into another. Once you've established a rhythm and have perfected your timing, you are ready to bring your cat into the picture and repeat these actions.

Initially, your cat may think that these tidbits are just random snacks. But pretty soon she will realize that it's a bargaining game. Once she does, you have in fact shaped a behavior.

Target. Click. Treat.

Target. Click. Treat.

Teaching your cat to perform tricks, such as shake paws, qualifies as feline enrichment—and quality time with your fur kid.

A total of five clicks and treats is a big training session for a cat who's new to the idea, so keep training sessions short—10 minutes at the most—and always quit while she's still interested. Your fur kid will learn faster this way. It's also important to hold your training sessions in different rooms to ensure that your feline will happily perform the behaviors you have taught her anywhere in the house.

The final step before you can get kitty to perform in front of an audience of family and friends is to remove the target altogether and get her to respond to a gesture or a verbal command. This will take some time and patience.

Sounds simple? It is. Any cat can be trained if you are prepared to take the time. Naturally, some cats learn faster than others. To make it even simpler, you can buy a special cat clicker training kit that includes the clicker, a packet of treats, and a booklet that outlines how to go about it. The kit also includes some fun ideas for activities that will bring both you and your feline many hours of fun and enjoyment. You can purchase one online at www.clickertraining.com.

STEPPING IT UP FOR THE ELDERLY

Remember, there will come a time as your cat gets older that she will no longer be able to jump up and climb on the furniture or the bed as she once did in her agile years. You will know when this happens because she will seek other places around the house in which to snooze instead. So when kitty needs help getting on and off the bed, it's time to buy pet steps and teach her how to use them.

It's strange, but that very same cat who was used to climbing the stairs in your home will eye the steps you've strategically placed alongside the bed or her favorite chair with suspicion and may possibly avoid them at all costs. More than likely, you are going to have to give her stair-climbing lessons.

It's quite easy. Stand her at the bottom of the stairs, and place a treat on a step just out of reach. Guide her up and allow her to eat the treat. Then gently help her up to the next step or two, and when she's reached her favorite spot, give her another treat and lots of praise. When she's mastered how to go up, reverse the whole process and teach her how to go down the stairs. She'll slowly get the hang of it, and I can guarantee that one day when you're not looking, she will climb up by herself.

When it comes to elderly kitties, feline enrichment empowers them to continue doing the things they enjoy, like getting onto the bed to snuggle with you. Your senior will thank you for allowing her to continue to be independent.

TOGETHER TIME

Whoever said exercising isn't fun has obviously never done it with a cat. While your fur kid will never really make a good exercise buddy if you are looking for a good calorie buster, you will definitely both limber up. Even as few as 10 to 15 minutes a day will bring positive results for your indoor kitty. Cats do enjoy playing in their kitty gyms or with their more elaborate toys, but they can have just as much fun batting a crinkled piece of paper back and forth with their favorite playmate—you.

Chapter Twelve

Lifestyles of the Furry and Fabulous: Home Accessories

I remember going to pet trade shows a few years ago and coming away disappointed because there wasn't much to see for cats apart from different-shaped sleeping cocoons and catnip-filled mice. My, how things have changed! A whole industry has now emerged focusing on our feline fur kids' well-being. In fact, feline enrichment is the new buzz phrase, and pet pampering has become a million-dollar industry. Statistics show that more and more pet parents spare no expense when it comes to keeping their pets happy and healthy.

THE LOWDOWN ON FELINE ENRICHMENT

Although cats have an innate talent to turn sleeping into an art form and seem quite happy to doze 23/7 (the remaining hour is for eating), boredom is in fact their biggest enemy.

Feline enrichment means providing your fur kid with the tools, if you will, to keep her both mentally and physically stimulated and to allow her to hone her natural instincts such as her hunting and fishing skills. It also means providing her with items of furniture that will allow her to climb and hide and generally spice up her indoor lifestyle, pique her curiosity, and entice her out of snooze mode.

By nature, cats are very playful and curious creatures. The smallest thing amuses them, and they can turn just about anything into a game. But because they look so content most of the time curled up sleeping, and because we lead such busy lives ourselves, we often tend to overlook their need for exercise and entertainment unless they initiate it.

There's no question that cats live longer, healthier lives indoors. But in looking after their welfare on this score, when it comes to hunting, playing, and generally amusing themselves, we have inadvertently cramped their style even more. We are turning these beautiful creatures into lovable but lazy old couch potatoes.

The situation is further exacerbated by the fact that because our own living spaces are getting smaller and smaller, we are forcing our cats to adapt to our shrinking indoor environment far too quickly. Some veterinarians believe that this is the cause of many medical issues, such as separation anxiety, extreme lethargy, and acid reflux, conditions that weren't previously seen in cats.

Kitty Feng Shui

Feng shui literally means "wind and water." It's the ancient Chinese method of creating a harmonious environment. It's about yin and yang, balance and harmony, and creating good energy in your home. But let's face it: Cats don't care which way the kitty condo is facing or where it's standing. From the feline point of view, feng shui is about giving your fur kid her own purrsonal space. It's about providing her with items of furniture that will allow her to climb and hide and generally spice up her indoor lifestyle, pique her curiosity, and entice her out of snooze mode. Kitty feng shui is about having lots of different toys that will keep her both mentally and physically stimulated and allow her to hone her natural instincts such as her hunting skills and fishing skills. It's about allowing your cat to be a cat.

Feline enrichment is definitely the cure for all these ailments. A busy cat is also less likely to be destructive around the home and will have an easier time staying slim and trim because feline enrichment can be equated with burning calories. Further, a busy cat is mentally stimulated, and as a result, socially more confident around people and other pets in the household.

PURRSONAL SPACE

Everyone needs their personal space in the home, and your cat is no exception. So apart from providing your fur kid with lots of stimulating toys and taking the time to play with her, feline enrichment can also be equated with giving your feline her own personal space.

The best part is that all this is very easy to do by adding a few accessories, such as scratchers, kitty condos, and kitty gyms. If you want to take it to the next level, you can expand her space with indoor ramps and runways and possibly give her access to a safe and secure outdoor area.

Just a few simple changes around the home can dramatically improve your cat's lifestyle. Relax! You're not going to need an architect or an interior designer, nor will you have to liquidate an investment to pay for it. As you improve your fur kid's life for the better, the benefits will rub off on you, too, because you will be automatically enhancing that inimitable human-feline bond.

THE ORIGINS OF FELINE ENRICHMENT

Before we get down to the nuts and bolts and create a blueprint for a kitty extreme home makeover, I would like to pay homage to the "pawfather" of what is now dubbed the Feline Enrichment Movement, namely photographer and cat lover extraordinaire Bob Walker. He and his talented artist-wife Frances Mooney live in a truly unique feline home in San Diego, California.

It started off innocently enough when Walker and Mooney noticed that their home was getting a bit cramped with eight adopted cats thundering around chasing one another and picking all the available human spots to snooze in most of the time. After visually surveying their abode, they realized that, like most people, they were thinking of their living space in terms of square footage. Cats, on the other hand, think in cubic feet because they enjoy high places and looking down on their people. So Walker and Mooney decided to experiment and incorporate the overhead space in their home into feline living and play areas.

Their first feline-friendly remodeling project was to create a floor-to-ceiling scratching column that also had the functional use of dividing their living room from the dining room. They entwined more than 395 feet (132 m) of red dyed sisal around it to lend it an artistic touch and then connected it to a wall-to-wall beam on their ceiling to give it stability. It was an instant success. The cats would run around the room, charging up the sisal wall and scratching to their heart's content. They also loved to climb up the column and perch on the top beam.

Walker slowly expanded the area by making holes in the walls and extending beams into other rooms of the house. Ramps and steps in different locations followed and linked more than 140 feet (46 m) of overhead cat walks. Finally, he boxed in corners of the room, creating inviting hidey holes to complete this ultimate arrangement of personal feline luxury space.

The media came and marveled. Manufacturers took notes. Walker and Mooney photographed everything and turned it into a best-selling book, getting the message out to cat lovers around the world. Without realizing what they had done at the time, they set the tone for much of the cat furniture and condos that enrich out cats' lives today. And to top it all off, they renamed their home "The Cats' House." These days, anyone can visit (by appointment) to get a firsthand look at the feline amusement park that improved their lifestyle, too, because it gave them back their favorite chairs.

I am sure that there isn't a cat on the planet who wouldn't love to live in the Walker home. But these days, it's easy to give your cat additional

Everyone needs their personal space in the home and your cat is no exception. Improve your fur kid's life for the better by providing scratchers, kitty condos, and kitty gyms throughout the house.

feline enrichment by borrowing from Walker's ideas or by going out and purchasing ready-made items that will help alleviate boredom and add excitement to your cat's life.

Today, feline furniture designers are very aware that whatever they create must fit in with our lifestyles and interior design trends. Not only are their designs in keeping with current styles, but they are bending over backward with their innovative concepts to help pet parents by outlining how their merchandise meets all the emotional, instinctual, and physical needs that enrich a cat's life. So you have no excuse!

SCRATCHING THE SURFACE

As already discussed, it's okay for cats to scratch. It's an instinctive feline trait. Cats usually aim for your favorite things because they're attracted to them by your scent. But before you rush off to inspect your fur kid's nails to see whether it's time for a trim, remember that you can keep her off your fine furniture and from swinging from your Thai silk drapes (cats are very attracted to silk—must have something to do with the silkworms!) by providing legitimate scratching zones and teaching her how to use them.

SCRATCHING PREFERENCES

The standard feline *modus operandi* upon awakening from snooze mode is to streeetch and scratch, scratch, scaraaatch! And just as we have our comfort zones and preferences, cats like things their way, too. The first thing you need to do is determine whether your feline prefers to exercise her feline scratching rights horizontally or vertically. Then, go out and purchase several scratching pads and posts to match her preference, and place them strategically around the house as close as possible to her most popular snooze zones.

SCRATCHERS

Scratchers come in all shapes and sizes—flat, angled, and the all-time favorite, vertical. Those that attach to a doorknob will allow kitty to put a bit of swing into the action. Scratchers that are raised like a ramp will provide endless hours of entertainment because she can somersault off and roll around as part of the fun. The nearest thing to Walker's wall of sisal is a scratcher that fits over the top of a door, giving kitty lots of

Location, Location, Location

Location and easy access are just as important as having scratchers your cat likes. And she is more likely to use it more often than your furniture if it's convenient for her to do so. Scratchers should be strategically placed where your cat will naturally spend most of her time:

- ❖ near the furnishings she likes to scratch
- ❖ near her bed and napping places
- ❖ anywhere you and your family spend time

If you need to convince your cat that the scratcher is indeed more interesting than your own furnishings, try sprinkling some catnip on it. If she enjoys catnip, it will make the scratcher a more enticing option. You can also try attaching a favorite toy to it or playing around it with a teaser toy.

When choosing a cat tree or kitty condo, look for designs that offer places to snooze and hide as well as a nice elevated lookout platform.

room to stretch and climb simultaneously.

If you are planning to get a vertical scratching post, make sure that it is not too short in height. It should be at least 3 feet (0.9 m) tall and sturdy enough to withstand a full-on attack when your cat is having a fit of the crazies and flying around the house.

Many people say that giving cats scratching posts covered in carpeting only encourages them to try and lift your wall-to-wall Berber in various places throughout the house. I have never really found this to be the case. However, my favorite material for vertical scratching posts is sisal. It's really strong and can withstand a lot of wear and tear.

The best way to introduce your cat to a new scratching post is to place a little catnip on it, which will automatically attract her. Alternatively, bring your fur kid over and start scratching at it yourself. You will be surprised how quickly she gets the message and takes over!

GETTING CREATIVE WITH CORRUGATED CARDBOARD

Recently, innovative interior designers have taken the feline need to scratch to a new level by designing an amazing array of feline furniture out of corrugated cardboard. Cats can then scratch, play, and snooze on these imaginative shapes. Style-wise, they fit in beautifully with any room of the home. Some of the bigger pieces shaped like loungers are strong enough to hold a person, too.

KITTY CONDOS AND CAT TREES

Because cats enjoy elevated positions, a multi-station kitty condo or a floor-to-ceiling cat tree is an essential feline entertainment center. Once again, not only will it keep her out of mischief and stop her from attacking things in the house, but it will be provide endless hours of amusement. Many kitty condos include scratching posts. If possible, look for a design that includes several and offers different surfaces, such as carpeting, sisal, and plain wood. On a side note, always be aware of splintering on a wooden post and occasionally take a piece of sandpaper and smooth it down.

Look for designs that offer places to snooze and hide, as well as a nice elevated observation platform. Many come with add-ons such as toys on a string and parts that twirl and swirl. If not, you can always add them yourself.

Many kitty condos come in kit form with instructions on how to set them up in numerous ways. If you really want to enrich your cat's life, you can take the condo apart from time to time and construct a different layout to keep things fresh and interesting.

KITTY AMUSEMENT PARKS

Depending on the space allowances of your home, the easiest way to create a kitty playground is to purchase two kitty condos and link them together with a plank. You can add on to your feline amusement park by taking certain other kitty items you have around the home and incorporating them into this main play station. For example, place a cat tunnel next to a circular hidey hole on the ground level of a kitty condo, and attach it on the other side to an ordinary cardboard box with holes cut out in it. To make the box attractive, you can paint it with nontoxic paint or even cover it with carpet tiles or fabric. Put your imagination to work! Your cat will reciprocate by using her imagination to invent some wonderful games. And of course, when she's had enough, she can retreat into the hidey hole and have a comfy snooze in the luxury of her own private getaway.

Hiding treats and toys in different places will rev up her curiosity and keep her permanently curious.

TAKING THE FUN OUTSIDE

It's a sad fact that cats living in urban areas face all kinds of dangers outside the security of their homes, such as attacks from other animals, traffic, and also the sheer cruelty of inhumane humans. In a perfect world, it would be wonderful if they could safely come and go and enjoy the great outdoors. However, it's still possible to provide your kitty with supervised access to an outside area to sun herself and nibble on fresh grass if you are able to construct an enclosure that she can access directly from inside your home.

I have a friend who, when remodeling her home, built a special cat door leading to an outside enclosure she calls her "kitty sunroom." It offers her cats the opportunity to bask in the sun and

Rules of the Great Outdoors

Many caring pet parents believe that cats deserve the right to roam, play, and sleep outside amidst the glory of their natural habitat. However, there are real dangers to the well-being and survival of a small, helpless feline in the wide-open spaces of the great outdoors.

Being hit by a car is one of the major causes of death for a cat who wanders outside without supervision. Other dangers, such as disease, parasites, predatory animals, weather hazards (sunburn and frostbite), getting stuck in a tree or caught in a trap, exposure to chemicals and pesticides, and freak accidents can prove hazardous to your feline's health, and quite possibly, her life.

As a responsible pet parent, make sure that your cat is never allowed outdoors without constant supervision. The safest options are to provide her with a safe outdoor enclosure or to take her out wearing a harness with a leash.

If you don't have a yard or have limited space, there are also prefabricated, portable enclosures available so that your cat can enjoy the outdoors on a deck or balcony in relative safety—as long as you are there to supervise. You can purchase these online from pet product websites and at some pet stores.

If you're handy, consider building your own outdoor enclosure or attaching one to your home.

snooze under the shade of a nice sturdy tree. It also has a patch of lawn, a sand pit, and fresh running water. The construction includes different shelves and posts for the cats to climb on and survey everything from different heights. The framework consists of heavy-duty steel that no other animals can access. And the floral creepers growing up the sides and over the top have turned the enclosure into a very attractive feature. At night, the cat door is securely locked and everyone sleeps soundly inside the house. I'm sure that any cat would give that a five-paw rating!

If you surf the Internet, you'll find many companies that construct special cat enclosures of all shapes and proportions. Of course, if you're handy, you can certainly make one yourself. These enclosures can be constructed anywhere: on a balcony, a patio, or even in a garden area alongside your home.

Personally, I am not a fan of portable freestanding structures that you put together yourself with poles and netting. I have never seen one that has passed my security test, and I would be afraid that a dog or wild animal could easily collapse it and possibly hurt or frighten any cat trapped inside.

If you have some outside space that is suitable to be transformed into an exterior play area, as well as some spare cash, your cat will definitely thank you. It's also interesting to note that many pet boarding facilities are now building special safe outdoor enclosures to allow their feline guests to experience the great outdoors. Some even include bird aviaries in their design so that felines can bird-watch from a distance. The best part is that many of them accept day visitors. So if you feel that your fur kid would enjoy a day of supervised outdoor entertainment, it can be arranged for a nominal price. It's the feline equivalent of sending your child to day care.

Be a purrfect pet parent, and let your cat live a little!

Many companies construct special cat enclosures of all shapes and sizes so that you can provide your kitty with supervised access to an outside area to sun herself and nibble on fresh grass.

Chapter Thirteen

Cats on the Go

You may be surprised to learn that 3 percent of felines travel with their pet parents every year. Now percentage-wise that may seem insignificant, but when you stop to consider that there are about 88 million cats in American households, that translates into around 2,640,000 felines on the go. If you include the number of show cats who travel the feline show circuits year-round, this number expands even more.

Cats are by nature homebodies, so the majority of pet parents opt to hire a cat sitter rather than book a pet plane ticket to visit Grandma for the holidays. But if you've ever considered taking your fur kid with you, it's certainly easier to travel with her than ever before.

CAT-FRIENDLY ACCOMMODATIONS

More than 20 years ago, singing legend Doris Day opened her famous Cypress Inn in Carmel, a beautiful area in northern California, and made dogs and cats welcome guests. In a sense, she created the blueprint that the hotel industry would later follow, and today some of the most luxurious hotels around the country are going out of their way to advertise themselves as pet friendly. And while many people consider pet friendly to be synonymous with dog friendly only, most hotel pet reception policies certainly include cats. At the Cypress Inn, cats are even invited to join guests while they enjoy a pre-dinner sherry around a roaring fire in the lounge.

These days, finding a nice hotel that will make your fur kid welcome is a mere mouse click away—there are numerous websites that detail what's available both countrywide and abroad. Apart from small boutique hotels and inns, don't overlook well-known hotel chains in all price ranges, such as Starwood Hotels, which also owns the W hotels; the Kimpton Hotel group; Ritz-Carlton hotels; Loews hotels; and the La Quinta Inn chain.

There are now many places designed to cater to people vacationing with their companion animals. Always call ahead to make sure your hotel or resort will accept pets.

FELINE AMENITIES

Pet travel has become such big business that in their quest for their share of the feline dollar, hotels are putting all kinds of services on a plate for the jet-setting fur kid. For example, on arrival at any W hotel countrywide, your fur kid will be greeted with a cat toy and treat, a W Hotel pet tag for her carrier, and a supply of litter cleanup bags. You will be given a welcome letter on her behalf with information about special pet services available through the concierge, including veterinary and grooming services, details about nearby pet stores, and a list of items available at the hotel's Whatever/Whenever store (which includes litter boxes, a Meow-Ow Box—a feline first-aid kit—and a variety of toys and treats). Upon arrival in the room, your pampered feline will find her own pet bed (you will have to persuade her to use it), a food and water bowl on a special floor mat, a pet-in-room sign for the door, and she will receive a special treat at turndown every evening.

If you check into any one of the stylish Loews' hotels, chances are she won't be eating the food you packed for her because the special pet room service menu offers some delectable chicken and fish dishes, all created by a special chef under the guidance of a veterinarian to ensure that they meet your pet's nutritional needs. Pet beverages include a variety of bottled water (which is usually much more comfortable on your pet's tummy while traveling) and milk. Also, if you prefer, a wide selection of both dry and canned pet food is provided. The Kimpton hotels all have doggie concierges that don't discriminate against feline guests; in fact, they're quite welcome to join in yappy-hour events held in the courtyards of most of the hotels throughout the summer months. There's a pet psychic on call if your feline is a little out of sorts, and the hotels also have a "Guppy Love" program—on request, they will place a goldfish in a bowl in your room for her amusement. Guests are kindly requested not to fish.

It goes without saying that any hotel that welcomes cats will be able to provide a responsible pet sitter at a moment's notice. Many have an affiliation with professional sitters in their area. Others even have pet sitters on staff. All you have to do is ask!

Some hotels charge a nominal pet fee. Others don't charge a daily room rate but request a cleanup deposit. Don't forget to inquire about special pet packages on offer, especially over holiday weekends such as Valentine's Day and Thanksgiving.

> ## *International Cat*
>
> I bet you didn't know that cats could say meow in different languages:
> - ❖ in America, it's *meow*
> - ❖ in Britain, it's *miaow*
> - ❖ in France, it's either *miaou* or *miaw*
> - ❖ in Italy, it's *miao*
> - ❖ in Germany, Spain, Finland, Lithuania, Poland, Croatia, Romania, Portugal, and Israel, it's *miau*
> - ❖ in Turkey, it's *miyav*

CRUISING THE HIGH SEAS

Cats on the water? Maybe. Generally, cruise ships do not allow pets on board. However, the Cunard line, which sails between the United Kingdom and the United States, has a special "Pets on Deck" program that will allow you to take your cat on the Atlantic crossing from New York to Southampton.

Cunard's flagship, the Queen Mary 2, has a state-of-the art kennel facility and a full-time kennel master to attend to your feline's every furry whim. And your fur kid will certainly be pampered en route with freshly baked cat treats, toys, a comfortable bed, and cat scratchers for her entertainment. All traveling pets get a special gift pack that includes a personalized name tag, a transatlantic crossing certificate, and a portrait photograph taken with you as a memento of the trip.

However, this doesn't strictly fall into the category of vacationing with your cat because animals are not allowed in the cabins or any of the public areas; they must remain strictly in the pet deck area, where pet parents can visit them. Such a cruise is a good alternative way of getting to Europe, though, if you prefer for your pet not to fly.

AIRLINE TRAVEL

If you are planning to travel by plane, you must ensure that your fur kid is booked on an airline that carries pets on an authorized travel route. You'll also need to know what rules the airline may have in place (and they can change, so check every time you travel), as well any restrictions the destination you are traveling to may have with regard to pets. You don't want to be left stranded if you are without proper documentation.

In fact, you should check all this out even before you handle your own travel arrangements. Certain airlines don't fly pets at all. Most carriers have temperature restrictions, so weather can dictate whether pets are allowed to travel. If the temperature is over 85°F (29°C), airlines will not fly your cat, and if it's less than 45°F (7.2°C), they require a letter of acclimation from a veterinarian stating that your fur kid can withstand the colder temperatures and that she's healthy enough to travel.

Make sure that your fur kid is booked on the same flight as you are so that you can personally see her board and be there to meet her on arrival. If she's traveling onboard with you, never give in to requests to take her out of the carrier at the security checkpoint. A nervous cat could bolt and disappear. Request to see a manager and ask to be taken to an enclosed room for the baggage search.

AIRLINE REQUIREMENTS

All the major carriers in the United States, namely American Airlines, Continental, United, Delta, Midwest, Northwest, US Airways, and Jet Blue, allow cats to fly in the cabin on domestic routes. But unfortunately, for international travel, your fur kid will have to travel in the cargo hold.

Each airline has its own specific requirements for crates traveling in the cargo hold and charge for the weight of the pet plus the crate. The crate has to be properly labeled to clearly state that it contains a live animal, and it must lock securely. Animals travel in a special air-conditioned cargo section. If you are traveling internationally, work with a pet travel agent who knows the ropes regarding individual airline requirements and all the necessary paperwork required, from health certification to other travel documentation. Check out a website such as www. puppytravel.com. If you leave it to the professionals, you can ensure that everything will be perfectly in place for your trip.

For up-to-date airline information, visit www.petflight.com.

FREQUENT-FLYER PROGRAMS FOR PETS

Yes, your fur kid can belong to a frequent-flyer program and clock up awards the same way you do. For example, on Midwest Airlines flights, cats are allowed to fly cabin class, so your fur kid can earn one free round-trip for every three paid round-trips

Every airline has its own rules about traveling with pets, so check before finalizing your plans.

that she flies with you as a member of the airline's Premier Pet Program. Midwest Miles offers a similar rewards program for pets. Members can redeem 20,000 Midwest Miles to get a free round-trip for a pet to travel under the seat in the passenger cabin and 15,000 for a pet to travel in the below-cabin pet compartment. Forms to sign your cat up are available at Midwest counters countrywide and are effective immediately. Visit www.midwestairlines.com for more information.

Other airlines offer great deals as well. EL AL Israel Airlines was the first international airline to introduce a frequent-flyer plan with its "Points for Pets" program in 2001. The airline flies from New York to Tel Aviv. After three trips in a three-year period, your pet can earn a free ticket. Japan Airlines has a program that operates domestically within Japan.

However, without a doubt, the leading contender in the field of international travel is Virgin Atlantic Airlines, with their "Passport for Pets" program. On their very first Virgin Atlantic flight, jet-setting fur kids are given a welcome onboard pet pack that includes a toy mouse called Red and a Virgin Atlantic collar tag. They are also given a special passport that records their flights but also allows them to collect paw prints, which they will be able to redeem for their gifts. One paw print

Foreign Travel With Pets

If you are traveling to a foreign country for vacation, you might not be allowed to bring animals into the country for various health reasons. Customs regulations may require your cat to remain in quarantine anywhere from several weeks to several months. Investigate the rules and regulations of traveling with a pet with your travel agent before making final arrangements.

is awarded per flight, and once furry travelers have collected five points, they become eligible for some of the fantastic goodies available. These rewards include things such as handmade Virgin bowls, plus a specially designed nonslip mat so that they can dine in style, or they can choose to donate their rewards to their favorite registered animal charity or sanctuary.

Alternatively, if they are feeling particularly loving toward their pet parent, they can donate 1,000 bonus air miles to their pet parent's Virgin flying club account. More individual gifts are available once the pet has flown 10, 15, or 20 times. They may receive blow-dries and pedicures from an upscale pet salon, pet clothing from Burberry, Prada, and Gucci, or even a personal pawtrait done by the famous English artist Cindy Lass, who is renowned for her paintings of the furry companions of celebrities around the world.

The "Passports for Pets" reward program is available on most Virgin Atlantic flights between American cities and the United Kingdom. For information, visit www.virgin-atlantic.com and search "pets."

GETTING YOUR FUR KID A PASSPORT

Some years ago, author Peter Gethers wrote several hilarious books about his travels to Europe with his Scottish Fold named Norton. Norton wined and dined in some of Europe's most fashionable restaurants and almost started a war in Italy over an uneaten sardine.

If you're planning to take your fur kid to Europe or Britain, she's going to need a passport. (The British Pet Travel Schemes (PETS) allows pets to travel freely from the United States to England and European Union countries.) Although the quarantine laws among the United States, Britain, and Europe have been removed, there's still a lot of paperwork to be done before your cat can fly.

There's a standard procedure to follow to apply for a passport for a furry traveler. In Europe, pets are issued a document that resembles an actual passport with their photograph inside. In the United States, the equivalent is just a paper certificate, but hopefully American felines will be able to acquire authentic-looking documentation in the not-too-distant future.

PASSPORT DOCUMENTATION CHECKLIST

To apply for a pet passport, your fur kid will need to meet certain requirements. She will need to be microchipped with an International Standards Organization (ISO) readable chip because tattoos and other forms of identification, such as standard ID tags, are no longer accepted as official identification.

She will also have to be vaccinated against rabies. Even if she has been vaccinated in the last 12 months, she'll need to be inoculated again. There is also a 21-day delay before a pet is allowed to travel because the veterinarian must show that the vaccination was successful on the travel documentation. Arrange a blood test with your veterinarian to take care of this well before your departure. Your traveling cat will also require booster shots.

It's a good idea to vaccinate your cat at the same time that you get the microchipping done because it means one trip to the vet. All the relevant paperwork will also have the same date, which will make travel documentation easier to keep track of. Make sure that your veterinarian includes all the following information on the paperwork:

- your cat's date of birth and age
- the microchip number, date of insertion, and location of the microchip on the animal
- the date of rabies vaccination
- the vaccine product name and the batch number
- the date booster vaccinations are due (this is calculated by reference to the vaccine manufacturer's data sheet)
- the date of parasite inoculation (if you are traveling to Britain, your fur kid will have to suffer the indignity of being treated against ticks and tapeworm; this has to be done 24 to 48 hours before departure)

All this preparation can only be done by a veterinarian accredited by the United States Department of Agriculture (USDA). Most veterinarians have this certification, but be sure to check.

The documentation then has to be sent to the appropriate government agency for final approval. Many veterinarians will do this on your behalf. If not, it's up to you to obtain approval. There is a charge for this, and it varies from state to state.

Some countries require all the information to be translated into their official language, too. Once again, be sure to check with their consulate office before traveling.

PACKING FOR YOUR CAT

To offer your fur kid the best possible travel experience, you will need to include some of her things on your travel checklist. By bringing a few familiar toys, litter, and food, you'll keep changes in her

To offer your fur kid the best possible travel experience, you will need to include some of her own things on your travel checklist such as food, litter, and some toys.

routine at a minimum so that she can feel a sense of comfort.

CHECKLIST OF TRAVEL ACCESSORIES

Whether you're flying or traveling by car, the pet industry has made life for the peripatetic pet very easy by pandering to the growing pet travel market and manufacturing a variety of feline travel items to make traveling with your fur kid relatively stress-free. Everything you will need for a pet on the go is available from pet stores and most definitely from pet catalogs and online stores. If you are shopping for a particular pet designer label for a carrier or other specific travel items, those manufacturers also have their own websites and will sell their wares directly to you online.

Carriers

A carrier is undoubtedly the single most important travel item. Many veterinarians endorse the idea that if cats are to travel by plane, it's less stressful for them to travel cabin class rather than cargo class. Unfortunately, as already stated, you don't have a choice if you are traveling internationally.

For airline travel, look for a soft-sided carrier that will fit under the seat and meet airline specifications if your cat accompanies you in the cabin. Never buy something simply because it looks pretty. Although airlines that accept pets on board are slowly beginning to standardize their requirements, it's still wise to check. Designs with roll-down flaps on the sides are great because cats like to hide and conceal themselves and will be much calmer if they are unaware of all the hustle and bustle associated with check-in. Then once on board, you can lift the flaps and let your pet realize that you are close by. Designs with lots of pockets are useful for papers and any travel necessities pertaining to your feline for the trip.

If pets are required to travel in the air-conditioned cargo section of the plane, as they will be for international flights, carriers have to be hard sided and made from wood, metal, or plastic material. Apart from the door, they must have ventilation on two sides and include a water container with outside access for filling in case a delay occurs. The carrier should provide sufficient room for your cat to be able to stand up and turn around. Actual kennel size allowances vary among airline carriers and the actual type of aircraft, so be sure to check. Most airlines will allow you to check two cats on a flight. It goes without saying that all transport carriers have to be well labeled and have secure luggage tags and escape-proof locks.

If you are traveling by car, the carrier you already own is probably fine. Any soft-sided carrier will work for road trips, but it's worth considering styles that double up as a sleeping cocoon at your destination. The round sleepy pods, as they are known, are something your cat will certainly enjoy. Some styles come fitted with a heating pad that plugs into the cigarette lighter in the vehicle, providing extra warmth during the trip. It's also wise to look for a design that can be secured with a safety belt for the duration of the ride.

I don't recommend carriers on wheels that resemble rolling hand luggage because your fur kid is going to be freaked out by every bump you encounter on the sidewalk as you wheel it along. By the same token, the shape of a backpack is uncomfortable for felines. Also, when people come up to you to try to pet her, you can't see what's physically going on behind your back.

Harness and Leash

If your cat is leash trained, you will be able to take her out and about for bathroom breaks, both while in transit and once you are at your destination. It's a good idea to leave the harness on for the duration of a road trip, which will allow you to simply attach the leash whenever necessary. This will make things less stressful for all concerned.

Invest in a really soft, comfy harness. I like the soft padded ones that are ostensibly sold for small dogs. They are comfortable and also offer pet parents the security of knowing that a cat can't wiggle out of it. Also, as I've mentioned previously, look for a design that closes on the top and not under the tummy. No cat will roll over and allow you to strap her in willingly. That's a dog thing!

Disposable Kitty Litter Boxes

Disposable kitty litter boxes are definitely the answer for any cat on the go. While most hotels will provide beds and bowls, they never provide litter, so it's a good idea to stock up on several disposable trays. It's not a bad idea to also put an extra container of litter in the trunk for unexpected emergencies.

Happy Travels

Familiarization is the key to happy travels, so purchase your cat's carrier well in advance and leave it casually lying around your home so that she can discover it for herself. You know how independent felines are—most will automatically snub anything new that you try to introduce. In this situation especially, self-discovery is the key to success. Allow your kitty to venture in for an investigation and snooze all in her own time. And you'll probably get better results if your cat's travel carrier is associated with fun stuff and never with a trip to the vet. Personally, I recommend a separate carrier for vet trips.

Disposable Feeding Bowls

There's a variety of different feeding bowls designed for travel. Bowls with lids are excellent for cats on a dry food diet. However, soft foods leave a sticky residue, so it's worth investing in a toss-and-go system of dishes. You can buy a special food bowl with a stack of disposable plastic inserts that you simply throw away after every meal. When meal times are fuss-free, it's far more enjoyable to travel with your feline. There are lots of different portable water bottles that convert into drinking bowls. Some even slot into the coffee cup area of a vehicle's console.

Sleeping Bags and Other Travel Paraphernalia

A roll-up pet sleeping bag is a great travel accessory for cats. You can roll it out and line the carrier with it, then use it as a sleep zone at your destination.

A window screen that suctions on to the window is an excellent idea to take along to screen out the hot sun. Because it's portable, you can move it around the vehicle throughout the journey. Don't forget to pack your feline's favorite toys and anything else she might like to have around that will add a note of familiarity.

A WORD ABOUT MEDICATION

If your cat is on daily medication, it's a good idea to buy one of those plastic boxes sold at pharmacies that allow you to portion out pills for a week at a time. Any medications that need to be refrigerated can be kept cold en route in a small thermal bag. Don't forget to pack syringes and droppers needed to dispense the liquids.

TRANQUILIZERS

To tranquilize or not to tranquilize—that is the question.

The most common tranquilizer used with pets who are nervous travelers is acepromazine. Others, including valium, are acceptable, but your vet will determine which one is best for your cat.

Significant tranquilization usually lasts about two to three hours, and then a gradual recovery occurs over the next few hours. If you're flying, it could be a problem if the medication wears off in flight, which will leave your fur kid very confused. And that's without taking any delays into consideration! Consequently, many veterinarians are suggesting spraying the carrier with a stress-reducing spray such as Feliway before takeoff. And don't forget that you can opt for a more natural alternative, such as Rescue Remedy. Again, all you have to do is add a few drops to the water bowl and then freeze it. This way, your pet can lick the ice as it melts and stay calm throughout the journey. You can do this for car journeys, too.

CHECKING IN

You have chosen your destination, prepared and packed appropriately, and are ready to enjoy a wonderful journey with your favorite fur kid. But you don't want to have a misstep once you get there.

Upon arrival, allow your fur kid time to settle in before you begin unpacking. Put down food and water and a kitty litter box immediately. Open her carrier door and allow her to come out in her own time and sniff around. Leave the door open so that she can access her carrier at any time. If you are traveling by car, it's a great idea to bring along an old scratching post and set it up close to her carrier. This will definitely help her feel more at home. A flat cardboard scratcher or one that hooks on to a doorknob is a great travel choice.

Pet parents now have the option to board their pets at luxury pet hotels and inns. These deluxe accommodations offer spacious suites, toys, special spa services, and personal attention.

When you leave your accommodations, put out the "Do Not Disturb" sign to discourage staff from entering and frightening your cat. It may also relax her if you turn on her favorite television show for entertainment and company.

If you take your fur kid outside of the room, be sure that she is wearing a cat harness she can't wriggle out of, and keep her on a leash. This is to protect her while being courteous to the other guests. Your other option is to transport her in a soft carrier to ensure her safety.

POSH PET HOTELS: BOARDING YOUR CAT

There will be times when your fur kid will be unable to accompany you on your travels. With the general boom in the pet travel industry, the days of utilitarian pet boarding establishments are over. These days, there are some fabulous all-feline hotels that will treat her with kid gloves. Personal recommendations from your veterinarian, friends, or groomer are always a good place to start.

Here's an idea of what you can expect. At places such as the Cat Hotel in Burbank, California, owner Sandy Rosker-Kelley is personally on hand to attend to every whiskered whim of feline guests. Your fur kid will probably rub noses with some celebrity cats because the hotel caters to a Hollywood clientele, which is always an endorsement of excellent pampering.

Don't Make Me!

If your cat really hates to travel and you're only going to be away from home for a day or two, you can safely leave her home alone if you arrange to have a pet-loving friend or neighbor visit periodically to check in on her. He can play with your kitty, make sure that she has enough food and water, and tend to the litter box. If you're going to be gone longer than that, make arrangements to check her into a pet hotel or hire a professional pet sitter to stay with her for the duration of your trip. Cats will become bored and lonely without companionship, human or otherwise, so it's important to provide for her comfort and proper care whenever you can't be with her.

As with all five-star establishments, 24-hour room service is available, with a snack menu offering cat treats, chicken, and cubed cheese. The cable television in the Queen Suites is permanently tuned to Animal Planet, and staff is on duty 24/7 to give plenty of hugs and attention on demand. The 37 kitty condo-suite hotel offers spacious duplex and tri-level lodging. Owners can choose a condo with a city view or a location close to reception, where pets can watch the bustling activity. Feline guests are allowed out of their condos one at a time to roam around the secure main floor, where they can climb the overhead beams and play or rest in the special cedar forest, where floor-to-ceiling cedar trees rescued from a burning forest are equipped with cushions and platforms.

At Camp Cat Safari, located in a beautifully remodeled turn-of-the-century building in Presidio Heights, San Francisco, a landscaped greenhouse offers feline guests the unique opportunity to enjoy the feel of the great outdoors from a safe enclosure. Surrounded by trees and plants, there are towers full of tropical fish and aviaries of twittering birds so that felines can look but not munch. And apart from the boarding facilities offered, owner Mark Klaiman encourages local cat parents to bring their felines for day trips to hone their natural hunting instincts and sit and watch birds.

Many other upscale establishments around the country offer themed suites with access to outdoor runs. Be sure to ask if they have webcams installed so that you can check in on your fur kid from wherever you are in the world. Many establishments do.

Always make reservations well in advance because many of these places are heavily booked with repeat business, especially over the holiday season and during peak weekends. Also be sure to ask about their vaccination policy. Most establishments will require proof of inoculations against rabies, panleukopenia (also known as distemper), feline rhinotracheitis, calicivirus, and pneumonitis (FVRCPP).

If your cat is on medication, explain what it is, what it is for, and how it should be given. Inquire if there is an additional charge for medicating. While most establishments have stylish pet beds and dinnerware, they are quite happy to let you bring your own, along with any toys or security blankets that will help your fur kid feel more at home.

PET SITTERS

The alternative to a cat hotel is getting someone to come and take care of your fur kid at home. Finding the correct pet sitter is no different than finding a competent person to take care of a child. Remember, just because people call themselves pet sitters doesn't necessarily mean that they are qualified for the job. If you are unable to get a personal recommendation, check the notice board at your vet's office. Alternatively, there are nationwide professional organizations such as Pet Sitters International (PSI) (www.petsit.com) and the National Association of Professional Pet Sitters (NAPPS) (www.petsitters.org) where you may find someone to meet your needs.

WHAT TO LOOK FOR

Whether you're working independently or with an organization, it's your responsibility to check each candidate's credentials. Before you agree to anything, it's a good idea to invite the prospective sitter over to meet you and your fur kid. Also, always ask for references. The Humane Society of the United States (HSUS) has drawn up the following checklist of points to cover at this initial meeting:

- ❖ Ask to see written proof that the pet sitter has commercial liability insurance to cover accidents and negligence, as well as written proof that he is bonded, which will protect you against theft (by the pet sitter).
- ❖ Inquire about what kind of training he has received.
- ❖ Ask for a written contract that spells out the services the pet sitter agrees to perform relating to your cat, such as an exercise routine, as well as other services, like bringing in the mail and putting out the garbage. Be clear about the fees involved. If it's a live-in arrangement, specify the times you definitely want the sitter to be with your pet. If it's not a live-in arrangement, familiarize the pet sitter with your home (light switches, entrances, etc.) so that he can easily check on your pet.
- ❖ Inquire if the person or organization has a backup plan in case of illness. Find out if the pet sitter is associated with a particular veterinary office or is willing to take your pet to your veterinarian.

It's important that the pet sitter understand your pet's temperament. Not all cats are outgoing and friendly toward strangers. And be sure to point out salient features of your home such as an alarm system and where you keep the remote control for the garage door.

Write out all instructions regarding your cat's food, medication, and general routine. Remember to pin up your contact information in a prominent place so that the sitter can reach you at any time.

It's also a good idea to give the pet sitter at least one neighbor's name and phone number and to leave an additional key with someone trustworthy in case your pet sitter gets locked out of the house.

OUTINGS CLOSER TO HOME

Travel doesn't only have to be associated with leaving home and heading to a far-off destination. If your fur kid is leash trained and not frightened by unfamiliar surroundings, she may enjoy going for walks around the neighborhood and even delight in exploring short hiking trails with you. You just have to be careful that she's not on too long a leash and can head off into bushes that are inaccessible to you. If that seems a bit too adventurous, consider a walkabout at an outdoor pet-friendly mall. The perennial problem regarding a cat on a leash is coming face to face with the unexpected, so always be wary of where you go with your pet.

On the other hand, I know a Bengal who likes strutting along the beachfront at Laguna Beach in southern California. She's totally unfazed by the skateboarders and volleyball players and is only too happy to be stopped and admired by strangers. It appears that the choice, as always, will be determined by your cat.

If your kitty is more of a homebody, a local social outing may be just the ticket. But that doesn't mean that your charming and talented feline won't be the center of attention! You can train her to do some party tricks that will amaze your friends and family—and be lots of fun for her, too.

A VISIT TO GRANDMA'S HOUSE

There's no reason why you can't take your fur kid on social outings if she is happy on a leash or in a carrier. She may grow to like the idea of accompanying her favorite companion (you!) if the conditions meet with her approval.

Pick a friend or family member who you visit regularly and who wouldn't mind a feline visitor. Often, people who don't have their own animals are only too happy to entertain a feline guest. And the more you do it, the more familiar the surroundings will become until your fur kid treats it as her second home. If this happens, *you* can get a bit territorial and leave a snooze mat, some toys, and some kitty litter for future visits.

Leash Training

What! You haven't leash trained your cat? Believe it or not, some cats will consent to accompany you on the end of a leash. Some even enjoy going out for regular walks around the neighborhood. You won't know until you try, right?

All you need are a leash and a harness—and a willing cat, of course. An H-shaped harness (not a collar) works well if the fit is snug enough. During training, go slowly and use lots of encouragement and treats.

Before you begin actual training, you must get your cat used to the idea of the leash and harness by leaving them around her sleeping area. Once she is accustomed to them being part of her territory, place the harness on her around mealtime (you can even persuade her by offering her something really special); when your kitty is very hungry, she'll be less likely to pay attention to it. Let her wear it for a day or two without trying to attach the leash to it.

Next, practice putting the harness on and taking it off for several days. When your cat appears to be completely used to the harness, attach a short leash to it and let her walk around the house with it on. She may fuss at first but will eventually accept it as an annoying but bearable appendage. Don't let your cat walk around unsupervised, however, because the leash could get tangled and possibly injure her. Next, try picking up the leash and following (not leading) your cat around. After all, you know you can't lead a cat! Again, you can use a small, delicious, smelly treat to persuade her to participate. You are now ready to take her out into the great outdoors.

COME ON,
LET'S STROLL

If your feline is not adventurous on a leash and you don't have a safe outdoor enclosure where she can enjoy some fresh air and watch the birds winging by, then it's a great idea to invest in a pet stroller in which to take her out and about.

I remember that there was a long silence when I announced to family and friends that I had bought my cat Cali a Jeep Wrangler for her 17th birthday. I guess those with vivid imaginations pictured us in a four-wheel-drive vehicle off-roading somewhere. So I had to explain that the Jeep in question was in fact a pet stroller made under license with the very same car manufacturer that makes cars for pet parents.

It is indeed a snazzy petmobile with front shock absorbers and rear safety brakes, and it offers pets a great view

If your feline is not adventurous on a leash and you'd like to take her out and about for some quality time with you, consider investing in a pet stroller. (The author and Cali.)

from a safe, mesh-enclosed interior. The ergonomic design offers comfort to both the passenger and the pusher. There's even a parent tray for water bottles and pockets for cell phones, keys, and other paraphernalia.

Fortunately, since I bought Cali her "wheels," other manufacturers have jumped on the bandwagon. There are now lots of fabulous designs to choose from, including ones that can be removed from their wheel base and converted into a standard handheld carrier. Most pet boutiques stock at least several models. Otherwise, you can shop online. There are websites that specialize in pet strollers, such as www.justpetstrollers.com.

Most cats who are able to enjoy a safe outdoor lifestyle like to hide under some greenery and watch the passing parade of insects and birds in the surrounding bushes and trees. You can give your fur kid the exact same experience from the comfort and security of a stroller. My felines were indoor-outdoor cats when we lived in Cape Town, South Africa. However, when we relocated to southern California, an indoor lifestyle was forced upon them because of the coyotes and bobcats that live in the hills surrounding our home. Both Cali and Fudge love outings in the stroller. I stick to paths in the neighborhood that are not usually populated by dogs, and they are very attentive of the passing scenery. It's one of the best feline investments I've ever made.

A TRIP TO THE MALL

Air-conditioned malls are great places for pet parents to go for some exercise out of the heat by walking and window shopping. Once again, if your fur kid has "wheels," there's no reason why she can't accompany you.

Unless you have a pet buggy comprising a carrier that fits onto a wheel base, you are going to have to transfer your fur kid from her carrier into her stroller. Once again, a word of caution: Don't risk it unless she is really easygoing in nature. If something spooks her, she could try to scramble out of your arms.

If your cat is fine for an outing at the mall, she will certainly enjoy a special outing to a pet store, where of course she will be more than welcome and possibly even spoiled with a fishy treat. Pet stores are a great environment to acclimatize cats to noise and other pets, especially if you are considering a career for your feline that will involve her being handled by strangers and around other animals.

Of course, visiting a pet store isn't just to go walking about; it's about shopping, too. Your fashionable feline can never have too many pretty collars (don't forget to purchase an identification tag, too) or too many toys. This is a great way to see what's new in the pet marketplace as well.

Then, naturally, you can break for lunch! Having a cat concealed in a stroller gives your fur kid privacy and also means that people may not mind that you have an animal companion at your table. Admittedly you will probably be seated in a pet-friendly outdoor area, but that's fine. Chances are your fur kid will snooze unless you are ordering something that smells particularly interesting!

TO GO OR NOT TO GO...

Although some cats may learn to enjoy traveling or being out and about, others have a harder time adjusting to it because they are accustomed to their routine home life. When forced to leave home, they may become anxious or stressed. Because of this, be mindful of what's best for your fur kid. She may prefer to be left at home or with a trusted family member or pet professional. Consider all the alternatives, and decide accordingly. On the other hand, if you have a jet-setting, well-traveled kitty, get going—happy trails!

Chapter Fourteen

Glamour Puss to Purrfessional: Getting Your Cat a Job

Once upon a time, the only job open to felines was that of resident mouse catcher. How things have changed! These days, many cats work in animal shelters, veterinary offices, and hotels as self-appointed receptionists and greeters. And some felines are just celebrities on the Internet.

*I*n addition to this, many pet parents have dreams for their felines: a movie career in Hollywood, a modeling job for magazines, or even a gig as a spokescat starring in television commercials for their favorite cat food. Others are happy to get their fur kids part-time jobs as pet therapists.

To be an official greeter in any kind of enterprise, a cat can rely solely on her outgoing personality and social skills, but a career in show business is definitely going to take some training, good people skills, and a great measure of good luck.

MAKING IT IN SHOW BUSINESS

Feline models and movie stars play a huge role in our popular culture. Remember Morris, the orange tabby spokescat for Purina's *9 Lives* cat food? Or Solomon, the white chinchilla who was the sidekick of Dr. Evil in the James Bond movies? More recently, popular cats on the big screen have included Mr. Jinks, who starred alongside Robert De Niro in *Meet the Parents* and *Meet the Fockers*, and Mr. Bigglesworth, the Sphynx cat who starred alongside Mike Myers as Dr. Evil in *Austin Powers*.

Every day, pet agencies around the country are inundated by doting pet parents with stars in their eyes determined to carve out a lucrative and visible career for their felines.

But before you let your fur kid give up her day job as the competent inventor of 101 different snooze positions on the family couch, know that stardom for your cat can be difficult to achieve. Just think of all those wannabe actors and models who have to struggle as waiters while they strive to turn a simple four-lettered word, namely "*work,*" from a noun into a very exciting verb.

Morris the Cat

Morris, undoubtedly the most famous cat in America, was a 14-pound (6.5-kg) orange tabby charmer who was rescued from a Chicago animal shelter by Bob Martwick, a professional animal trainer. He became spokescat for Purina's 9 Lives cat food in 1969 and eventually became honorary director of StarKist Foods with power to veto any cat food flavor he didn't like. He was invited by President Nixon to cosign (with a paw print) the National Animal Protection Bill.

The problem with getting your cat started on a successful show biz career is that most cats don't have the level of training needed to cooperate on a project over a lengthy period. And on a typical movie set where there may be hundreds of people being paid top dollar by the hour, no director is going to put up with feline tantrums. Consequently, as with any business, when it comes to employing felines on a movie or television set, production companies and photographers tend to rely only on highly trained professionals.

THE LOOK

Any feline look is popular in the movies and on television, and your cat doesn't necessarily have to have an amazing pedigree as part of her resume. Often, film directors use more than one cat in a role. Cats with unusual markings don't often get parts in films because their markings make it more difficult to get a feline body double. Black cats are rarely used because it's difficult to capture their facial definition on film.

FINDING WORK

Seek out local photographers in your area and ask them whether they ever work with animals, cats in particular, of course. You may even consider having a set of professional photographs taken for future use, similar to the head shots talent agencies require of human actors.

When it comes to employing felines on a movie or television set, production companies and photographers tend to rely only on highly trained professionals.

Some photographers have connections and may be able to set up an appointment with a pet talent agency. If so, set up an appointment and come prepared with a resume, photos, and a reel if you have one. (That's a collection of clips from prior projects your cat has starred in or a really professional video shot at home.) If your cat has no prior experience, some agencies may be willing to give you an interview to assess her potential.

You can see if there are any photographers or pet talent agencies in your area by surfing the Internet. But be wary of anyone who asks for money and offers nothing in return.

TIPS FROM AN AGENCY TRAINER

Fees for television or movie appearances are negotiated according to the skills the cat is trained to perform. Aside from being well behaved and easily trainable, your feline will have to be able to react to hand signals because talking is not allowed on the set during shooting. She will also have to have a very placid nature. Filming a single scene can take time!

You may want to check out local advertising agencies or film schools and make them aware of your feline's abilities in front of the camera. All film students need to make a movie to graduate, and this is a great way to get your feline into the business. She could earn quite a bit of money once she gets some solid professional experience.

IT'S ALL ABOUT TRAINING

If you are serious about being a stage mom, then you are going to have to clicker train your cat so that she has a large repertoire of commands and tricks that she can perform. Approach pet talent agencies in your area and find out what training classes they have to offer.

Remember, in show business, success has a great deal to do with luck, and because it's so competitive, another famous Hollywood maxim also applies: It's not what you know but who you know.

THE COMPETITIVE EDGE: A CAREER IN THE SHOW RING

After spending so much time pampering your cat, and I'm assuming you've now read this book from cover to cover and put into practice every suggestion on these pages, you may begin wondering what it would be like to compete in a cat show.

Remember that the show ring isn't the exclusive domain of pedigreed felines. Cat shows include a household section that is open to mixed breeds—and that means every beautiful cat on the planet. In this category, cats are judged collectively without regard to their sex, age, color, or coat length. Instead of being judged to a specific breed standard, the competitors are judged for their uniqueness, pleasing appearance, unusual markings, and sweet natures. The only rule is that they may not be declawed, and if they are more than eight months old, they must have been spayed or neutered.

Your cat fits the bill, right? Well, there's nothing to stop her from trying to win a few ribbons. In fact, every cat entered receives a red and white merit award as a testament to her good health and vitality. I have never entered Cali or Fudge—they are so gorgeous it would be unfair to their competition!

Before you download an entry form from the Internet, remember that being a show cat mom or dad is quite a commitment. Whether your fur kid is pedigreed or a mixed bundle of charisma, start by being truthful with yourself and answer the following questions:

- ❖ Do you have the dedication to learn how to groom your cat for the show ring? This is particularly important if she is pedigreed and going to compete in the arena.
- ❖ Do you have the patience, time, and determination that it takes to be a show cat mom or dad?
- ❖ Do you like to travel?
- ❖ Most importantly, how do you think your cat will react? Will she enjoy competing?

Lots of people who show professionally say that their cats don't mind the travel and thrive on the attention, both in the show ring and from spectators. Your fur kid's temperament is the key to your success in the show ring.

GET ADVICE FROM THE PROS

If you're not sure if *you* are ready for the ring, remember that going to a cat show can be a spectator sport, too, and perhaps this is the best way to find out if you and your feline have what it takes. Show cat moms and dads are usually willing to share information and are happy to chat, as long as you are mindful that they are there to compete. Education and grooming workshops are always held at these shows, and attending will certainly give you insight into how it all works.

As far as your fur kid is concerned, you are going to have to gauge how she reacts when held by others and whether bright lights and noise affect her adversely. If she does a Marlene Dietrich number and wants to be alone whenever you have guests, rushing upstairs to snooze under the bed, take it as a clue that perhaps she may not enjoy a career in the spotlight after all.

PET THERAPY CATS

Maybe being that type of crowd pleaser isn't your kitty's bag, but there are other ways she can contribute her talents to good ends. In recent years, there has been mounting evidence that all pets are a tonic to human health, lowering stress, reducing blood pressure levels, and adding to our general sense of well-being. Consequently, there has been a rise in the number of animals visiting patients in hospitals, with increasing verification that they can play a significant role in shortening a patient's recovery time.

The Delta Society, based in Bellevue, Washington, is a world leader in the field of human-pet relationship research. Through their Pet Partners Program, volunteers and their animals are trained to visit patients in schools and health-care environments. They are also trained to work with children who have learning disabilities and in a variety of other programs such as drug and alcohol rehabilitation.

It takes a special cat to be a therapy cat. For starters, she must enjoy being around people and be willing to be held and sit in laps to be petted for long periods. Cats can sign up with any family member, including children, to be part of an official pet therapy program. Enlisting your fur kid as a pet therapist is a wonderful way to do volunteer work and spread the joy that a feline can bring to people who are unable to have a cat permanently in their lives.

Enlisting your fur kid as a pet therapist is a wonderful way to do volunteer work and spread the joy that a feline can bring to someone who is unable to have a pet permanently in his or her life.

There are many animal-assisted therapy programs around the country. The best way to find out what is in your area is to contact the Delta Society or ask your veterinarian.

Cats are truly amazing and intuitive creatures, and a well-socialized feline can be very loving and comforting to strangers. By involving your cat in therapy work or even just taking her to visit an elderly or sick person you know personally, you are spreading that love, making someone's day and the world a better place.

A GLAMOUR PUSS AT HOME

Well, you ask, what if your glamour puss is a die-hard homebody? Although she's looking absolutely furbulous, she'd rather just stay away from all the lights, cameras, and action and hang out at home simply impressing you. It looks like the only way you can document her furbulousness is to take out the camera and capture your top cat in some picture perfect poses.

CAPTURING THE MOMENT

Today's point-and-shoot digital cameras are definitely a cat's best friend. They are simple to use and lightweight enough to keep in your pocket or purse, which means that you'll always be ready to catch those magic feline moments—like the time Fudge was sitting next to the computer screen looking very bored because I wasn't stopping to scratch and pat. Suddenly, she yawned—something she always does twice in quick succession. I was ready and captured the second yawn. Bingo!

The fun part of having a digital camera and a library of great feline camera angles on file is that they can be used in so many wonderful projects that are fun and easy to do. With a few clicks and a computer, you can even turn your fur kid into an international star because there are many cat websites where you can post photographs. There are also books and calendars that invite submissions. The possibilities can provide endless fun. And your cat won't even have to leave home!

I'm not going to take you through a Photography 101 course. There are plenty of books and actual courses for that. My focus is on capturing your favorite feline around the home, doing what she does best—to capture those magic moments that we all want to freeze in time forever.

GUIDE TO PHOTO SUCCESS

There is one very simple rule for success. Always have your camera ready, and be prepared to take lots of shots to build up a portfolio. The "snooze-or-you-lose" maxim certainly applies when it comes to photographing felines. Time waits for no man, and neither does a cat!

But there's a precursor to being camera ready, and that's buying the right camera and getting to know its features well. Fortunately, there are many digital cameras on the market that cater specifically to the technically challenged—like me.

Here are a few features to keep in mind when you go shopping:

* Many of the newer-model digital cameras don't have viewfinders, so you are relying solely on viewing your subject on the LCD screen. Be sure to buy a camera with a big screen. Don't buy anything smaller than 2.5 inches (6.4 cm); 3 inches (7.6 cm) is even better. It's much easier to capture those magic moment when you don't have to squint!

* Check the camera's internal memory capabilities. Most of them don't offer much space, which means stocking up on memory cards at the time of purchase to ensure that you don't run out of space.

* Check to see if the camera comes with a rechargeable battery. Digital cameras can be hard on batteries, which can get expensive.

* Make sure that the camera has an image stabilization function.

* Most importantly, check to see if the camera has photographic enhancement technology that will improve the quality of your shots for you.

* Video capabilities are a nice feature, too. This means that you can share your cat's antics with your friends and the world via YouTube.

* Test various cameras to see how easy it is to access the different features before you buy.

Once you've made your decision, put your cat on your lap and read the manual. And be sure to commit all its special features to memory. Then, take your cat off your lap and get ready to begin.

FOLLOW THE BOY SCOUT RULE: BE PREPARED

It is sadly an unknown author who summed up our irresistible fascination with felines with this quote: "In ancient times cats were worshipped as gods; they have never forgotten this."

And *you* have to remember this because cats don't pose on command. In fact, they rarely respond to their name beyond a mere flick of the tail, and they never take direction from photographers—even professional ones!

So if the first rule of success is to

When photographing your fabulous feline, the first rule of success is to always have your camera close at hand—the second rule is to have lots of patience!

always have your camera close at hand, the second rule is to have lots and lots of patience. When I am going through a photographic phase and want to add photos to my collection, I keep my digital camera on my desk because that's a place my cats love hanging around. Consequently, I have managed to capture some great shots simply by being camera ready and knowing my pets well enough to anticipate when they are about to have an "attack of cute."

BACKGROUNDS CAN MAKE OR BREAK

It's often better to take the background to the cat than the cat to the background. In other words, if your feline has a favorite spot like the top of your couch, place the background cloth or throw you want to use in the photo on her favorite spot, and apply a liberal dose of patience until she gets used to having it there.

You can use either a plain or truly interesting patterned fabric, but keep the area clear of clutter. The idea is to show off your cat's fur color to its best advantage.

GETTING DOWN

Get down to your fur kid's level, even if it means lying down on the ground. This is a great way to also learn about your feline's world from her perspective. She doesn't have to be looking directly at the lens for you to capture a great shot. Just keep snapping!

Further, experiment with interesting angles by moving around your subject. Stand on a chair and shoot directly down. Lie on your back under her kitty condo and try to capture her peering over the edge of one of the ledges. Don't be rigid; move your camera to capture both vertical and horizontal shots.

Positioning your cat in different places in the viewfinder, either one- or two-thirds across the screen, will instantly create an interesting composition.

IT'S ALL IN THE LIGHTING

As any professional photographer will tell you, it's all about the lighting. Here are some good basic rules to follow.

* If your cat is an indoor cat, try to position her so that she is bathed in natural light. However, don't put her directly in front of a window because you'll black out her features and create a silhouette. And be aware that a flash can give felines green eyes, the equivalent of red eyes in humans. Use the red-eye reduction mode on your camera.

* If your fur kid is leash trained and you are able to take her outside for a photographic session, the best light is a bright overcast day because you won't get shadows spoiling your shots. Planning a photographic session for early morning or late afternoon will also work well for similar reasons. If the sun is shining, try to keep it behind you.

* Use the flash outdoors, too, to help erase shadows. (Check the flash range of your camera.)

- If your fur kid is on a leash, try to conceal it so that it doesn't end mid-air in the shot.
- Wherever you're shooting, remember to experiment with your zoom lens. Zooming in close will help limit background distractions and give you lots of lovely detail.
- Lock the focus to get a sharp picture. Simply push the shutter button halfway down, make sure that you are happy with what you see in your viewfinder, and then press down completely.

PROPS AND TREATS

Whether your cat is clicker trained and will respond to a target or you are winging it in the hope of capturing some really interesting shots, it's a good idea to work with an assistant to dispense treats and work with props. All cats will respond to visual stimuli such as a laser beam or their favorite feathered toy on a wand. Even a piece of string will create some lively actions and reactions.

SHOW YOUR CAT IN ACTION

Cats love to play, and it's fun to capture them in action. Single-lens reflex (SLR) cameras, either digital or film, are better for action photography than the standard pocket digital. If you are using film, use a high-speed (400 or 800) film to stop the action. Plan for the action to happen in one spot, and then focus there.

MAKE A MOVIE STARRING YOUR CAT

If your digital camera has a video feature, use it to make short three- to four-minute videos. There're lots of places on the Internet where you can post your work and reach a large, appreciative audience. After all, it's fun to share with other doting cat lovers.

If you happen to own a video camera, have some fun and set it up on a tripod focused on your cat's favorite spot. A colleague of mine set up her camera in front of her feline's favorite pink fluffy bed and just let it roll until the tape ran out. The final edited result showed the cat arriving and climbing onto her bed and falling asleep undisturbed as other animals in the household thundered past, doorbells rang, and people came and went. The cat, an orange tabby (nice

Special Effects

Here are some special tricks to use when photographing your cat:

- Put some catnip around your camera lens. That will "reel in" your feline for some fun and quirky close-ups.
- If you have more than one cat, rub a bit of butter behind one of their ears, and they will automatically look as if they are kissing and cuddling.
- If you have a glass-topped table, place your cat in the center and watch what happens. Most cats will freeze in position. Put a marker on the glass, and focus on it before you put your cat in place. (Try shooting from underneath as well.)

By keeping a visual diary in photos or on film, you can preserve some wonderful memories of your feline companion to cherish for a lifetime.

contrast on the pink bed) was so fast asleep, she fell off and had to climb back up on the bed again. It's truly hilarious footage.

The Kitty Diaries

Another fun idea is to create a visual kitty diary simply by filming a chronological list of events that highlight your fur kid's life.

If you are about to adopt a kitten or a cat, the opening footage can depict visits to various animal shelters leading up to the magic moment when you find your feline soul mate. Scenes such as signing the adoption papers and coming home can follow. This kind of video calendar is not too demanding because you can pick up your camera where you left off and add footage at any time.

Remember, other events that relate to your cat are also worth including, such as your first visit to the pet store to buy food and choosing a beautiful collar. Don't forget kitty's first birthday and general family occasions and holidays such as Thanksgiving. Most cats will appreciate a turkey tidbit!

Some Helpful Hints

Before making a video, study some television advertisements that feature cats. For example, take your favorite television cat food commercial and count the number of different shots that make up the entire spot. To make your footage look more professional, borrow techniques such as switching angles often. Don't film from one angle for longer than about ten seconds. When you zoom in, count to five and do the same count when you zoom out. Practice makes perfect!

Remember, the days of the silent movie are over. Titles and even screen credits at the end, along with appropriate music, will make your footage very professional. There are lots of computer programs available that will help you add these finishing touches. However, if you are technically challenged and unable to edit, don't panic too much. After all, this is a home movie and not a submission to the Academy of Motion Picture Arts and Sciences. Or is it?

And remember, many of the same rules pertaining to still photography apply, such as making sure that you are eye level with your feline to capture the action from her perspective. Don't forget to use toys and treats, too.

FINAL TIPS FROM A TRUE PURRFESSIONAL

Jim Dratfield of New York City is my favorite pet photographer. His photographs capture the essence of that special bond between pets and their people, and his attention to detail turns them into truly magnificent works of art. No wonder the rich and famous from all walks of life, from statesman Henry Kissinger to fashion designer Ralph Lauren and movie stars Jennifer Anniston and Laura Dern, commission him to portray their pets on photographic paper.

Fortunately, he's listed in my address book under "Special Friend," and he kindly obliged with some professional hints and tips.

❖ Work with a partner and create a human backdrop. Sit your assistant (someone the cat knows and loves) in your cat's favorite chair, and cover the assistant with a piece of fabric from the shoulders down to the ground. Then position the cat on this background. When you are ready to shoot, simply get your assistant to lean back and lift his hands out of the picture. You can technically improve the composition by cropping afterward.

❖ A neutral fabric like a dark gray or brown works well. But you can also try using an interesting piece of fabric or a piece of tapestry so that it becomes part of the beauty of the photograph.

❖ If you are working alone, contain your fur kid in a room where you can close the door and there are no items of furniture to hide under because this adds stress if your feline keeps leaping off and hiding.

❖ Line your kitchen or bathroom sink with your background fabric to create a contained place to keep your feline still for a couple seconds—hopefully long enough to shoot. If she has a favorite chair but it's in the wrong position in the room in terms of natural light, move it to a better lighting location and leave it there until she gets used to the new position. Then get your camera out.

❖ Get your assistant to hold a piece of string or plastic wrap in front of the lens, and whip it away when you are ready to shoot. This will give the impression that your feline is looking directly at the lens. Tuna or catnip captures feline attention, too!

Dratfield doesn't believe in primping the cat before a photo shoot; he loves to capture them *au naturale* and endorses the lots of patience advisory. "You want your cat to be relaxed so that you don't get that deer-in-the-headlights startled look. Cats are very honest in their response to a camera. And because they never truly pose, you can capture some powerful images."
Thanks, Jim!

Now go capture some magic moments so that you can admire your fabulous feline and preserve a lifetime of wonderful memories.

Chapter Fifteen

Beauty Secrets From Fabulous Show Cats

You know what it's like, we all read celebrity magazines in the hope of gleaning a few hints and tips from the beautiful people—how do they outline their lips to make them look plump and full without Botox; how do they apply mascara so that their lashes don't stick together in a clump; what's the secret to beautiful tresses that never loose their bounce?

eline pet parents are no different. For many cat lovers the sheer pleasure of attending a cat show is simply to get up close and purrsonal with these glamour pusses and perhaps learn a few tricks of the trade to try out on their own felines at home—even if they have no aspirations of ever showing their fur kids.

Fortunately, the owners of some of the country's top champions weren't catty or territorial about keeping their little tricks to themselves. In fact, they were very willing to share their prized beauty secrets exclusively in these very pages. So take special note.

Fabulous Beauty Secret #1: Static Control

To remove static from a cat's coat, finely spray the fur with mineral water. It removes the static that plagues fur, especially in dry, wintery weather. It also keeps fur moisturized for a brilliant sheen.

From Persian Grand Champion, Grand Premier National Winner WiccaCats Krystalle Lynn; owned by Jean Dugger of Atlanta, Georgia

Fabulous Beauty Secret #2: Staying Fresh During Travel

When traveling by car, place a wet towel in the carrier to provide a source of moisture and to reduce static in the fur.

From Japanese Bobtail Grand Champion Kyattsuai Yufako; owned by Mary Newmarch of Milwaukee, Wisconsin

Fabulous Beauty Secret #3: Kitty Saunas

Run a hot shower to steam up the bathroom, and then take your cat in there with you. You can even leave her in there after you leave—but only for a few more minutes. Don't let her overdo it in the kitty sauna! This is an excellent and easy way to add moisture to the fur and remove static in extremely cold climates.

From Abyssinian Grand Champion Nepenthes Nereus, ranked fourth best cat at the 1979 CFA Best Cat National Awards; owned by Joan Miller of San Diego, California

Fabulous Beauty Secret #4: Tearstain Removal

To remove tearstains around the eyes (especially on longhaired and light-furred felines), wipe the entire face using a washcloth or a thick paper towel soaked with warm water. Dab the area with a liquid tearstain remover, and then brush it with the same product in powder form. Finally, apply a hypoallergenic human eye shadow to the area with a large makeup brush in a color that blends with the fur.

From Persian Grand Champion, Grand Premier, National Winner WiccaCats Krystalle Lynne; owned by Jean Dugger of Atlanta, Georgia

Fabulous Beauty Secret #5: Bright Eyes

Keep the hair on your cat's upper lid well trimmed to prevent hair from falling into her eyes and causing excessive tearing.

Wipe the eyes with a saline solution for sensitive human eyes, and then apply colloidal silver drops, a natural antibiotic available from health stores in a 10ppm (ten parts per million) solution as follows: one to two drops per eye, one drop per nostril, and two drops in the mouth. This can be done several times a day. The solution can also be added to the water bowl. This antibacterial measure lessens tearing and thus reduces staining.

From Cream Point Himalayan Grand Champion Felindia's Hearts of Fire; owned by Gail and Jackie Ogden of Marietta, Georgia

Fabulous Beauty Secret #6: Color Touch Ups

To touch up stains and faded fur, apply a special pet chalk stick available in a variety of fur colors directly onto the fur and comb it through. For the hocks, rub the hind legs with chalk. Lightly comb the area, and apply a colored grooming powder that will coat the fur.

From Japanese Bobtail Grand Champion Kyattsuai Yufako; owned by Mary Newmarch of Milwaukee, Wisconsin

Fabulous Beauty Secret #7: Fur Guard

To keep fur clean while eating, use coffee filters as a bib. Simply cut a hole in the middle for your cat's head. They are easy to make, cheap, and disposable.

From Cream Point Himalayan Grand Champion Felindia's Hearts of Fire; owned by Gail and Jackie Ogden of Marietta, Georgia

Fabulous Beauty Secret #8: Getting Big Hair

To add volume and fullness to the coat, use a wire brush and blow the hair in the direction opposite to the way it grows—the same way some hairdressers do with long tresses at the salon. Finally, blow dry in the correct direction to make it full and fluffy. This works very well on longhaired cats.

From Persian Champion WiccaCats Belladonna Lynne; owned by Jean Dugger of Atlanta, Georgia

Fabulous Beauty Secret #9: Wet-Hand Grooming

Put a few drops of water on your hands, rub the coat backward, and then start stroking it in the direction the fur falls. This wet-hand grooming technique will remove dead hairs and add moisture to the fur. Also, the natural oils on your hands will add a finishing gloss to the coat. This tip works extremely well for shorthaired cats.

Further, if you are planning a career in the show ring for an Abyssinian cat, always groom entirely by hand because combs will pull out the live hairs and brushes will flatten the coat. Bathe your cat about a week before a show to allow the natural oils to give the coat a lustrous look.

From Abyssinian, Grand Champion Nepenthes Akime, Best Abyssinian and ranked ninth in the 1980 CFA Best Cat National Awards; owned by Joan Miller of San Diego, California

Fabulous Beauty Secret #10: High-Gloss Sheen

To degrease a coat and add a glossy sheen on shorthaired cats, finely grind oatmeal in a blender and apply the powder to the coat. Use a rubber comb to gently work it through the hair. Then use an ordinary car chamois cloth and wipe the coat. The more you wipe the coat with the chamois, the glossier the sheen. Preground oatmeal flour purchased from a store is just as good.

From Natural Mink Tonkinese Kittentanz Musky; owned by Bill and Michelle Harrison of Jasper, Georgia

Fabulous Beauty Secret #11: Calming Poufy Fur

To calm poufy fur, use different shampoos in succession. Start with a degreasing shampoo. Then apply a moisturizing shampoo to the fur tips. Finally, apply a volumizing shampoo throughout the coat. For the final rinse, use a weak solution of vinegar and warm water to make hair squeaky clean. (Be careful not to use too much vinegar in the solution because it can irritate skin and dry out the fur.)

From Blue Point Himalayan Persian Grand Champion Burnbrae's Jordan; owned by Lyn Knight of Mount Airy, Maryland

Fabulous Beauty Secret #12: Squeaky Clean Fur

For squeaky-clean fur, take 1/4 cup of white vinegar and dilute it with 1 quart of warm water for a final rinse to remove any traces of shampoo. Then keep rinsing with ordinary water to remove any traces of the vinegar rinse.

From Oriental Shorthair Grand Premier Kat-Attack's Ricochet of SlinkInc; owned by Jill Abel of Denver, Colorado

Fabulous Beauty Secret #13: Tidy Top and Tail

For a tidy top and tail, make a paste using cornstarch to degrease hair around the ears and the tail. Apply the paste with your fingers or a cotton ball. Let it dry for 10 to 15 minutes, and gently comb out. It works really well and won't leave a gritty residue.

From Japanese Bobtail Grand Champion, National Winner Wyndchymes Tess; bred by Mary Newmarch of Milwaukee, Wisconsin

Fabulous Beauty Secret #14: Adding Highlights

To add sheen to a dark brown or black coat or to accentuate the markings on a tabby or tortoiseshell coat, mist the fur with an aftershave called Bay Rum, which is made from original bay rum oils from the Virgin Islands. It works wonders and smells great, too!

From Scottish Fold Grand Champion, National Winner Kitjim's Brairpatch, Distinguished Merit (1981–1997); owned by Kitty Angell of The Woodlands, Texas

Fabulous Beauty Secret #15: Grooming With Style

Whatever you're spraying on the coat, whether it's mineral water, aftershave, conditioning sprays, or calming spritzer, never spray directly on the fur or on a comb. To groom with style, mist above the cat and allow it to drift down and settle on the fur. Then rub it in with your hands and gently comb.

From Havana Brown Grand Champion, Regional Winner Soesthill Charlie Pride; owned by Anne Edwards of Rolla, Missouri

Fabulous Beauty Secret #16: Glamour Puss Regimen

For a real glamour puss, change shampoos regularly depending on where you live and the time of year—just like people do. Use more than one type of shampoo during a bath to treat the skin and add luster and shine to fur. Never use a shampoo that contains dye on a black coat. During the bathing routine, use a cotton swab dipped in mouthwash to remove excess oil from the inside area of the ear tip. (Never use it in the ear canal.)

From black Persian Grand Champion, Breed Winner, National Winner Catsafrats Shine On voted Cat of the Year in 2003; owned by Donna Isenberg of Culver City, California

Fabulous Beauty Secret #17: Plush Coats

To add density and plush to a coat, wet the fur with a damp cloth. Spray a finishing spray in the air and allow it to mist down. Run your fingers through the hair backward, and allow the fur to dry naturally. This will make the coat appear really thick—if you touch it, you can leave a handprint.

From Russian Blue Grand Champion, Regional Winner Kay Brook's Prince Charming; owned by Kay Janosik of Minneapolis, Minnesota

Fabulous Beauty Secret #18: Texturizing Fur

To keep hair smooth over the thighs and to ensure that it doesn't part, spray a texture spray (available from grooming-supply stores) on your hand and rub it onto the fur. Blow on the fur with short breaths as you comb the hair. This technique straightens and smoothes.

From Japanese Bobtail Grand Champion Kyattsuai Yufako; owned by Mary Newmarch of Milwaukee, Wisconsin

Fabulous Beauty Secret #19: Dandruff Remover

To deal with temporary dandruff and other specks on a black coat, put a couple drops of mouthwash on your hands, rub it over your palms, and gently run your hands over your cat's fur. This tip is particularly useful to help make shelter cats look more glamorous and hence easier to adopt.

From Abyssinian Grand Champion Nepenthes Akime, Best Abyssinian, ranked 9th Best Cat, National Awards, 1980; owned by Joan Miller of San Diego, California. As a show judge and head of the Cat Fanciers' Association's Outreach and Education Program, she does a lot of demonstrations showing shelter volunteers how to groom cats to make them more presentable to hopefully be adopted quickly. This is a tip she uses all the time to combat temporary dandruff that's often caused by nervousness or dryness in the air.

Fabulous Beauty Secret #20: Polishing to a Sheen

To add polish and sheen to fur, brush the coat with a rubber curry brush (purchased at cat shows or special pet-supply stores) to draw out dead fur. Then use a chamois cloth to give the coat a glossy sheen.

A dry washcloth is also great for removing superfluous dust that's noticeable on a black coat.

From Cat of the Year 2004, Bombay Grand Champion, Breed Winner, National Winner, Caricature's Colin Powell; owned by Sharyn and Sig Hauck of Sarasota, Florida. Colin Powell, the cat, actually met his namesake, General Colin Powell, former Secretary of State, in Washington, DC.

Fabulous Beauty Secret #21: Accentuating Natural Highlights

Cats such as Bengals have a pelt that glistens in the sun. To accentuate these natural highlights, mist the cat with a sheen spray and rub her down with a grooming glove.

From Bengal Champion Mainstreet Kashika of AngelTree; owned by Karen Anderson of Orange County, California

Fabulous Beauty Secret #22: Purrfect Skin for Hairless Kitties

If you have a hairless kitty, the best way to ensure that she has a perfect nonoily skin is to embark on a regular beauty routine similar to what you would do for your own face. Use a soft exfoliating mitt to remove dead cells, and then bathe your cat using a soap-free baby shampoo to remove excess oils. This is an essential beauty routine—otherwise, your fur kid could leave an oily imprint in her favorite sleeping spot. Alternatively, you can use specially formulated cat wipes all over her body. Don't forget to also wipe between the toes and inside the ears.

From Sphinx Grand Champion, National Winner and Cat of the Year 2006 Majikmoon Will Silver With Age; owned by Dee Dee Cantley of Los Angeles, California

Fabulous Beauty Secret #23: Tomcat Tamer

If your tomcat seems besotted with every queen he meets, put him on estrogen pills before a show or photo shoot, with the advice of your vet of course. It will keep him focused on himself, and he'll forget about girls for a while!

From known playboy Japanese Bobtail Grand Champion Kyattsuai Yufako; owned by Mary Newmarch of Milwaukee, Wisconsin

Fabulous Beauty Secret #24: How to Be a Celebrity Show Cat

If your cat is planning a modeling career in front of the camera or in the show ring, get her used to noise and activity by leaving the television on during a loud and noisy football game; if she can handle the voiceover announcements and the cheering, she'll be a natural. Also, take your cat out and about to pet stores on a leash, and get her used to meeting and greeting strangers.

From Bengal Champion Mainstreet Kashika of AngelTree; owned by Karen Anderson of Orange County, California

AUTHOR'S FABULOUS RESOURCE LIST

- Cat Fancy, the world's most widely read cat magazine, has a website that is an excellent general resource for everything feline; go to www.catchannel.com
- Most veterinarians who only see cats in their practice are members of the American Association of Feline Practitioners (AAFP); go to www.aafponline.org
- If you want to find a holistic practitioner in your area, go to the American Holistic Veterinary Medical Association's website at www.ahvma.org
- American College of Veterinary Behaviorists provides a list of board certified behaviorists at www.dacvb.org
- American College of Veterinary Dermatologists offers helpful information and resources at www.acvd.org
- American College of Veterinary Ophthalmologists has a special website for the public at www.acvo.org/publicframe
- Veterinary Oral Health Council lists health dental treats on their website www.VOHA.org, and a list of veterinary orthodontists is available on the American Veterinary Dental College website www.AVDC.org
- The National Association for Holistic Aromatherapists provides a list of therapists operating around the country at www.NAHA.org
- If you are unsure which flower essences would be best for your cat under particular circumstances, Bach Flower remedies offers an on-line consultation service by emailing consultation@bachflower.com
- To learn about pet massage and other therapies, visit AMTIL (Animal Massage & Therapies) at www.AMTIL.com
- To learn more about Zoopharmacognosy, the study of animals selecting aromatic plants for health and healing purposes, visit www.ingraham.co.uk
- The Cats' House. You can visit this unique cat playground in San Diego, California by appointment. Contact Bob Walker at www.thecatshouse.com
- To learn about Karen Pryor's cat clicker training methods, go to www.clickertraining.com
- To find out more about cat agility training and tournaments, contact International Cat Agility Tournaments (ICAT) at www.catagility.com
- The ASPCA's website, www.ASPCA.org, provides a comprehensive list of nontoxic edible plants as well as a list of toxic plants; the ASPCA Animal Poison Control Center hotline is an excellent resource for all poison-related emergencies. You can also reach them by phone 365 days a year and 24 hours a day at 1-888-426-4435 365.
- The Cat Fanciers Association website, www.CFFA.org, is a great resource to learn about different cat breeds from fur type to temperament
- The International Cat Association (TICA), one of the largest genetic cat registries worldwide, can be contacted at www.tica.org
- The British Pet Travel Schemes (PETS) allows pets to travel freely from the United States to England and European Union countries; to learn more about how to get your cat a passport to travel, go to www.defra.gov
- For questions relating to cat adoption and general shelter information, contact the Humane Society of the United States at www.HSUS.org
- If you're planning to travel with your cats, get updates on cat-friendly accommodations at www.petswelcome.com and www.takeyourpet.com

To learn more about pet therapy programs around the country, contact the Delta Society at www.DeltaSociety.org

INDEX

ABOUT THE AUTHOR

Sandy Robins is an award-winning pet lifestyle writer. Her work appears in many national and international publications, as well as on popular websites such as MSNBC.com and MSN.com. She hosts a pet travel segment called *Pets on the Go*, which is featured on the syndicated radio show Pet Talk With Harrison Forbes and also writes a cat lifestyle column for *Cat Fancy*, the world's most widely read cat magazine. She lives in California with her family, including her fur kids Cali and Fudge.

PHOTO CREDITS

Gregory Albertini (Shutterstock): 125
Galyna Andrushko (Shutterstock): 50
Anyka (Shutterstock): 66
Ngo Thye Aun (Shutterstock): 52
Joellen L. Armstrong (Shutterstock): 25
Joan Balzarini (Shutterstock): 63, 150
Andrew Barker (Shutterstock): 147
Peter Baxter (Shutterstock):171
Charlie Bishop (Shutterstock): 72
Tony Campbell (Shutterstock): 138
HD Connelly (Shutterstock): 86
Laurent Dambies (Shutterstock): 33
Hermann Danzmayr (Shutterstock): 55
Geoff Delderfield (Shutterstock): 99
Bairachnyi Dmitry (Shutterstock): 64
Sebastian Duda (Shutterstock): 126, 176
Anna Dzondzua (Shutterstock): 163
Isabelle Francais: 142, 144
David Gilder (Shutterstock): 16
Stefan Glebowski (Shutterstock): 1, 88
Johanna Goodyear (Shutterstock): 6, 90
Ben Heys (Shutterstock): 122
Shawn Hine (Shutterstock): 48
Indigo Fish (Shutterstock): 9
Ingret (Shutterstock): 166
Eric Isselee (Shutterstock): 181, 182
Ivanov (Shutterstock): 93
Rene Jansa (Shutterstock): 131
Aki Jinn (Shutterstock): 81
Elena Kalistratova (Shutterstock): 58
Robert Kirk (Shutterstock): 112
Kochergin (Shutterstock): 128
Koriolis (Shutterstock): 39
Erik Lam (Shutterstock): 26, 169, 183, 184
Larisa Lifitskaya (Shutterstock): 136

Linda Z (Shutterstock): 173
Ovidiu Lordachi (Shutterstock): 18, 119
Linux Patrol (Shutterstock): 17
Tatiana Morozova (Shutterstock): 70
Mark William Penny (Shutterstock): 68
David Pruter (Shutterstock): 36
Lee O'Dell (Shutterstock): 43
Jeff Oien (Shutterstock): 29
Alvaro Pantoja (Shutterstock): 159
Zoltan Pataki (Shutterstock):107
Robert Pearcy: 40, 116
Michael Pettigrew (Shutterstock): 74
Olaru Radian-Alexandru (Shutterstock): 178
Sandy Robins: 115, 164
Robynrg (Shutterstock): 10, 13
Ronen (Shutterstock): 105, 121
Ruzanna (Shutterstock): 58
Pavel Sazonov (Shutterstock): 15, 85, 94, 102
Weldon Schloneger (Shutterstock): 82
Christopher Sista (Shutterstock): 79
Fernando Jose Vasconcelos Soares (Shutterstock): 148
Spauln (Shutterstock): 4
Spring (Shutterstock): 96
Lara Stern: 108
The Supe87 (Shutterstock): 47
Mariusz Szachowski (Shutterstock): 60
TFH Archives: 12, 21, 23, 31, 45, 76, 80, 111, 153
Simone van den Berg (Shutterstock): 57
Antonin Vodak (Shutterstock): 156
Monika Wisniewska (Shutterstock): 101
Daniela Wolf (Shutterstock): 35

Cover: Stansilav Popov (Shutterstock)
Back Cover: Erik Lam

DEDICATION

To my beloved parents Ed and Rennette Robins, who taught me to love and respect all creatures great and small. Tragically, they died in a fire on December 23, 2007, just days before this manuscript was completed. Daddy, you will always be on my shoulder looking out for me.

ACKNOWLEDGMENTS

When it comes to acknowledging the amazing behind-the-scenes help I received with this manuscript, I am faced with the problem of having to list someone first and someone last. Such is the nature of a list! Everyone mentioned deserves the same equal praise and heartfelt thanks. You all took my phone calls and never suddenly switched me over to voicemail. No one changed their telephone number or email address either! Thanks to my best friend Gail Alswang who, when this manuscript turned into a sea of words, helped me sail through it. Susan Logan, Cat Fancy magazine's amazing editor, has been a guiding light and truly understands that these days cats have a lifestyle too. Dr. Jill Richardson of the fabulous website Zootoo.com (formerly chief guru at The Hartz Mountain Corporation) willingly shared copious amounts of information and gave me some excellent contacts like feline groomer extraordinaire Erica Salvemini, owner of the Just 4 Paws Mobile Pet Spa. Linda Healy, Lone Area Trainer for Petco, has trained hundreds of groomers to work with cats countrywide and happily imparted knowledge. Feline specialist Drew Weigner has always gone out of his way to educate me, and so has veterinary dental specialist Dr. Jan Bellows and veterinary ophthalmologist Dr. Michael Brinkmann. My own fur kids are lucky to have Dr. Jeff Glass as their purrsonal veterinarian. I wish I could clone him! I take far better photographs thanks to the Kodak Eastman Company and pet photographer Jim Dratfield. Cats are far better off since Karen Pryor educated cat lovers about how to train our felines. My home has stunning plants that my fur kids can nibble on ever since Nancy Matsuoka of Laguna Hills Nursery in Laguna Hills, California taught me about edible gardening. Thank you to Bach Flower Remedies for allowing me to publish their list of flower essences, which benefit cats, and to Caroline Ingraham of the Animal Aromatic Science and Research Centre in the United Kingdom, who explained just how clever cats and other animals are at finding plants that will help heal them. To W. Bruce Bregenzer, thank you for teaching me about animal massage therapies. Nicky Bunzl, my self-proclaimed personal assistant in London, continues to send me interesting feline stories and ideas. Thank you to Allene Tartaglia, Executive Director of the Cat Fanciers' Association and to Joan Miller, Director of the CFA's Outreach and Education Programs, who I had on speed dial, for fielding dozens of questions with excellent answers and for giving me great contacts to get the beauty secrets from celebrity show cats that make this book so special and unique. This project wouldn't have happened without Erin Niumata and Jeff Kleinman of Folio Literary Management. I am privileged to be in their fold. My husband Mike Sandler is a perennial fountain of savvy business advice and support. Finally, thanks to my beautiful tortie cat Muffin (birth unknown – January 12, 2005), who walked into my life one cold and rainy night back in 1994 and stayed to warm my heart forever. When she got an invitation from her veterinarian Dr. Jeff Glass in 2004 inviting her to enjoy some spa treatments to destress after a long illness, the idea for this book was born.

A big "thank you" goes to Mary Grangeia at TFH Publications who was initially listed in my address book under "E" for Editor but is now listed under "F" for Friend.

And finally, to my coauthors Cali and Fudge, who munched treats and snoozed for hours on end while I slaved away at this manuscript. You make my world purrfect.

PRAISE FOR *FABULOUS FELINES*

"I dare anyone to look at this book and not admit cats are the most beautiful creatures on the planet. Of course, cats are well aware of this fact. Here, they've divulged their beauty secrets to Sandy Robins. Seriously, even experienced family members owned by cats (after all, we know cats own us) will benefit from the practical advice and cutting edge information. Truth is, there are lots of handy dandy dog tip books, but few with such high quality focusing on fabulous felines. I love this book more than my cat loves catnip."
Steve Dale, Cat Behavior Consultant; Host, *Pet Central*, WGN Radio, and nationally-syndicated radio show *Steve Dale's Pet World*; Contributing Editor, *USA Weekend*; Nationally Syndicated Columnist, Tribune Media Services

"*Fabulous Felines* is a must-read for every cat lover and a must-have for every cat owner!"
Jai Rodriguez, Host, Animal Planet's *Groomer Has It;* Host, *Queer Eye for the Straight Guy*

"*Fabulous Felines* is a delight to read, yet so practical. Readers will enjoy Sandy Robins' witty style and their cats will benefit from her wisdom."
Susan Logan, Editor, *Cat Fancy*; *Cats USA; Kittens USA;* CatChannel.com

"*Fabulous Felines* breaks new ground spotlighting the enormous array of innovative beauty, grooming, and fitness trends and treatments that focus on feline well-being! A must-have for any cat owner who wants to pamper his or her favorite fur kid with a fabulous lifestyle and the utmost in good care."
Marty Becker, Resident Veterinarian, *Good Morning America*; Veterinary Contributor, *The Martha Stewart Show*

"Thoroughly entertaining, enjoyable, informative and very interesting; to be read and re-read by all cat lovers everywhere! I thought I knew everything there was to know about with cats. But lo and behold was I surprised! Some very original ideas. Thank you for this lovely book."
Donna Isenberg, The Cat Fanciers' Association

"*Fabulous Felines* reveals how to pamper your feline friend with a fabulous lifestyle while offering the very latest and best in care, grooming, and fitness fun written in Sandy's inimitable and very readable style."
Harrison Forbes, Host, *Pet Talk With Harrison Forbes*; Pet Behaviorist, *Live With Regis and Kelly*

"*Fabulous Felines* is loaded with great information and advice that every fabulous pet parent needs. Robins' expertise, humor, and fondness for felines flow through every page. I loved it!"
Nancy Peterson, Feral Cat Program Manager, The Humane Society of the United States

"Everything anyone wants to know about the care of felines. In a word: fantastic. Whiskers from Blossom Street would approve."
Debbie Macomber, *New York Times* Best-Selling Author

"*Fabulous Felines* is a must-read for any cat lover. The book is chock full of helpful tips and easy-to-follow instructions to keep your cat beautiful. Bathing cats doesn't have to be stressful to your cat or dangerous for you when you follow this book's helpful instructions. From bathing to nail clipping, this book has all the answers to the questions you have about kitty beauty care. It's a great reference for any cat owner who wants to keep their glamour puss happy and healthy."
Jill A. Richardson, DVM, *Zootoo.com*

"A feline pampered in the delightful manner described in *Fabulous Felines* is a treasured kitty indeed! A wonderful blend of kitty facts and pampering hints on how best to care for your feline fur kid."
Linda O. Johnston, Author, *Kendra Ballantyne, Pet-Sitter Mysteries*, Berkley Prime Crime, including *Meow Is for Murder*